In the Name of the Salish & Kootenai Nation

The 1855 Hell Gate Treaty and the Origin of the Flathead Indian Reservation

"It being understood and agreed that the said confederated tribes do hereby constitute a nation under the name of the Flathead Nation."

--Treaty with the Flatheads, etc., 1855

In the Name of the Salish & Kootenai Nation

The 1855 Hell Gate Treaty and the Origin of the Flathead Indian Reservation

Edited by
Robert Bigart
and
Clarence Woodcock

Published by
Salish Kootenai College Press
Pablo, Montana

Distributed by
University of Washington Press
Seattle & London

Library of Congress Cataloging-in-Publication Data:
In the name of the Salish & Kootenai nation : the 1855 Hell Gate
    Treaty and the origin of the Flathead Indian Reservation / edited by
    Robert Bigart and Clarence Woodcock.
        p. cm.
        Includes index.
        ISBN 0-295-97545-8 (paper : alk. paper)
        l. Salish Indians—Treaties. 2. Salish Indians—Land tenure.
3. Salish Indians—Government relations. 4. Kutenai Indians—
Treaties. 5. Kutenai Indians—Land tenure. 6. Kutenai Indians—
Government relations. 7. Confederated Salish and Kootenai Tribes
of the Flathead Reservation—History. 8. Flathead Indian
Reservation (Mont.)—History. I. Bigart, Robert. II. Woodcock,
Clarence.
E99.S2I5 1996   96-4730
978.6'832—dc20   CIP

ISBN 0-295-97545-8 (paperback)

Salish Kootenai College Press publishes books and pamphlets relating to the history and culture of the Salish and Kootenai Tribes and
Flathead Reservation affairs. Manuscripts have been chosen because
they include valuable information that should be more widely available. The views expressed are those of the authors.

The editors would like to dedicate this work to our parents and to those values of justice and respect for others we learned from them.
Robert Bigart
Clarence Woodcock

This book is published with the assistance of a generous grant in the memory of

Bradley Robert Brazill
(1964-1994)

He was a very special young man and an heir to the 1855 Salish treaty makers. Bradley's kind and generous spirit touched many lives. He especially enjoyed honoring his Salish heritage through traditional dancing at the powwows.

Picture Credits

National Anthropological Archives,
Smithsonian Institution, Washington, DC.
  Drawings by Gustavus Sohon.
    Victor, Neg. #37,417
    Moise, Neg. #37,417-A
    Ambrose, Neg. #37,416-B
    Adolphe, Neg. #37,417-C
    Insula, Neg. #37,416-A
    Bear Track, Neg. #37,417-D
    Pelchimo, Neg. #32,876-H
    Thunder, Neg. #37,416-H
    Pacha, Neg. #37,417-E
    Alexander, Neg. #37,417-B
    Michelle, Neg. #37,417-H
    Bonaparte, Neg. #37,416-F
    Choits-Kan, Neg. #32,876-F
    Broken Leg, Neg. #37,416-D
    Pierre, Neg. #32,876-J
    Louis Ramo, Neg. #37,417-F
    Pagh-Pagh-Sem-i-am, Neg. #32,876-G
    Iroquois Peter, Neg. #37,416-C
    Iroquois Aeneas, Neg. #37,416-G
    Charles Lamoose, Neg, #37,416-E
    Flathead Indians Playing Ring, Neg.
      #37,644-J
    Flathead Treaty Council, Neg.
      #37,644-G
Washington State Historical Society, Tacoma,
WA.
  Drawings by Gustavus Sohon
    Big Canoe
    James Delaware
Isaac I. Stevens, "Narrative and Final Report of
Explorations for a Route for a Pacific Railroad."
In *Reports of Explorations and Surveys for a
Railroad Route From the Mississippi River to the
Pacific Ocean*. vol. 12, book 1, House Executive
Document No. 56, 36th Congress, 1st Session
(1860) serial 1054.
    Flathead Lake, Looking Southward,
      p. 178.
    Hell Gate—Entrance to Cadotte's Pass
      From the West, p. 244.
    Fort Owen—Flathead Village, p. 122.
    Bitter Root River Near Fort Owen,
      p. 250
    Victor's Camp—Hell Gate Ronde, p. 127

Entrance to the Bitterroot Mountains,
  p. 180
Kamas Prairie of the Pend d'Oreilles
  Indians, p. 178.
Hot Springs at Source of Lou Lou Fork
  Bitter Root Mountains, p. 180.
John Mullan, *Report on the Construction of a
Military Road From Fort Walla Walla to Fort
Benton*. (U.S. Government Printing Office,
Washington, DC, 1863)
    Mode of Crossing Rivers by the
      Flatheads and Other Indians,
      p. 50
    Pend d'Oreille Mission in the Rocky
      Mountains, p. 52.
K. Ross Toole Archives, Mansfield Library,
University of Montana, Missoula.
    Isaac Ingalls Stevens, Picture 76-1179.
John C. Ewers, *Gustavus Sohon's Portraits of
Flathead and Pend d'Oreille Indians, 1854*.
Smithsonian Miscellaneous Collections, vol.
110, no. 7 (1948).
    Gustavus Sohon, frontpiece.
Oregon Province Archives, Gonzaga University,
Spokane, WA.
    Adrian Hoecken, S.J.
National Archives, Washington, DC
    First page of original Hellgate Treaty
    Signatures from original Hellgate
      Treaty
Montana Historical Society, Helena, MT
    John Owen

Map Credits

Stevens Treaty Expedition 1855
    David L. Nicandri, *Northwest Chiefs:
    Gustav Sohon's Views of the 1855
    Stevens Treaty Councils* (Washington
    State Historical Society, Tacoma, 1986)
    p. 6.
Tribes and Historical Locations of Western
Montana
    Map by Marcia Bakry, Smithsonian
    Institution, Washington, DC,
    1973.

Table of Contents

Message from the
Kootenai Culture Committee

The oral evidence from Kootenai Indian elders indicates that the Kootenai delegates to the council played a much more active role than the government transcript indicates. This may be because Michelle, the Kootenai chief, coordinated his position at the talks with Alexander, the Pend d'Oreilles chief. Much of Michelle's input would have been in discussions among the Indian leaders. Then Alexander presented his and Michelle's position to Governor Stevens as recorded in the official English transcript from the National Archives.

The oral tradition also shows that the Indian leaders had a different understanding than Stevens did of some of the terms of the treaty. Much of the oral information has yet to be gathered from the elders and analyzed in detail. The concepts of selling land and the exclusive ownership of natural resources by a few people were new and strange ideas to the tribes. A special study urgently needs to be done to examine the treaty from the tribal viewpoint.

Examining the tribal perspective on the treaty will add a new and very important dimension to the history of the 1855 Hell Gate Treaty.

Kootenai Culture Committee
of the
Confederated Salish & Kootenai Tribes
Elmo, Montana
November 1995

Editors' Note

The material in this book was limited by what was available. The reader should remember that these studies represent the views, biases and interests of the individual authors.

The two most glaring weaknesses in these studies of the Hell Gate Treaty are the lack of a study of the oral evidence of tribal elders and the need for a detailed evaluation of the evidence of how the United States government carried out its responsibilities under the treaty.

The Postscript of this book reprints some letters from the National Archives which raise serious questions about the federal government's first payment of $36,000 to the tribes. Much of the initial payment in 1860 was in the form of overpriced, poor quality, and unneeded merchandise.

There are many ways to spell Pend d'Oreilles, Kootenai, Hell Gate, and other names used in the text. IN THE NAME OF THE SALISH & KOOTENAI NATION has preserved the spellings used in the manuscript originals or earlier publication of these materials resulting in some inconsistencies between articles.

If IN THE NAME OF THE SALISH & KOOTENAI NATION stimulates study and discussion within the Flathead Indian Reservation community, the book will have been successful. The treaty and its importance on the reservation should foster further studies that could help expand the viewpoints expressed by these authors.

Robert Bigart
Clarence Woodcock

On September 30, 1995, Clarence Woodcock died at his home in St. Ignatius, Montana. I am thankful to have been able to work with Clarence on IN THE NAME OF THE SALISH & KOOTENAI NATION and other projects. I am sad to loose a friend, but appreciate the opportunity we had to share our interests in research and writing about Salish Indian history.

Robert Bigart

In the Name of the Salish & Kootenai Nation

The 1855 Hell Gate Treaty and the Origin of the Flathead Indian Reservation

Introduction

On July 16, 1855, eighteen leaders of the Flathead, Kootenai, and Upper Pend d'Oreilles Indians hesitantly signed an agreement with the United States Government. The government negotiator for this historic document was Isaac I. Stevens, the ambitious 37 year old governor of Washington Territory. Born of confusion and disagreement, the treaty was one of the most important legal documents in Western Montana history. It provided the legal foundation for the relationship between the Confederated Salish and Kootenai Tribes and the federal government and established the Flathead Indian Reservation.

The treaty was signed at Council Grove near modern Missoula, Montana. The Indian people at the council expected to discuss the establishment of peace between the Salish and Kootenai and their encroaching enemies, the Blackfeet, not land cessions. Poor interpreters and conflicting cultural values regarding the land and the economic future of the tribes, prevented the council from becoming a true meeting-of-the-minds. In addition, Governor Stevens was short-tempered and haughty in his dealings with some of the Indian speakers at the council. Stevens had established a tight timetable for his summer's work of permanently settling the "Indian question" in Washington Territory, and he had no time for Indian leaders who wanted to discuss the cession in a more thorough manner.

Few of the participants in that troubled council could have guessed how important the treaty they signed would be in influencing the course of Western Montana history:

● The treaty set the stage for forty years of confusion over the Salish claim to the Bitterroot Valley.

● It allowed the tribe to fight efforts by government bureaucrats to "close" the reservation in the late nineteenth century and forbid Indian people from leaving the reservation without an agency pass.

● It was the basis for the tribes' objection to the opening of the reservation without tribal consent in 1910 since the treaty stated that the reservation was for the tribes' "exclusive use and benefit."

● Article 6 of the treaty contained the ultimate sleeper clause. This clause included by reference an article from a treaty with the Omahas which was distorted in 1904 to imply Salish and Kootenai consent to individual allotments and the sale of so-called "surplus" lands to whites.

● It guaranteed the right of the Salish and Kootenai people to continue to hunt and fish in their accustomed territory.

● It established the federal government's obligation to supply certain basic educational, medical, and economic assistance to the tribes.

● It has served as the principal legal basis for the sovereignty of the modern Confederated Salish and Kootenai Tribes.

The treaty was important for the federal government because in it the tribes ceded their title to almost all of the land in Western Montana except the present Flathead Reservation. The treaty clearly spells out that the reservation was the portion of the tribal homeland which the tribes declined to give up to the federal government, not a gift from the federal government to the tribes—a grant from the tribes, not to them. The treaty also provided a framework for peaceful official dealings between the tribes and the federal government.

As most Indian people on the reservation are careful to point out, the treaty represents an agreement entered into by two sovereign parties. While the translation problems may cloud the consent given by the tribes, there is no question that the federal government fully understood the terms of the treaty. Consequently, most people would agree that the treaty should not be modified or altered in any way without the freely-given approval of the tribes.

Legal Interpretation of Indian Treaties.

Over the years the federal courts have realized that special language and cultural problems surrounded the negotiation of treaties such as the Hell Gate or Council Grove Treaty of 1855. In explaining the terms of the treaties to the Indians, historical sources have frequently indicated that the government negotiators did not secure competent interpreters and did not take the time to make sure the Indian people really understood the agreements. Yet the courts must now rule on the meaning of the treaty based on the English version.

Because of these problems the courts have developed a number of basic principles which they use to guide the interpretation of Indian treaties. Among these principles are:

(1) Ambiguous expressions in treaties should be resolved in favor of the Indian tribes.

(2) Treaties should be interpreted as the Indians themselves would have understood them.

(3) Indian treaties should be liberally construed in favor of the Indians.

The application of these principles in a given court case will depend on the facts in that individual case.

In general, the courts have been careful to consider the treaties as grants from the tribes to the government. The tribes are assumed to have been fully sovereign or independent bodies when they made the treaties. By virtue of the treaty, the tribes became a "domestic dependent nation" under federal Indian law, and retained all powers not given up by the treaty, an act of Congress, or federal Indian law. Congress can change the terms of a treaty without the consent of the tribes involved as a result of a 1903 Supreme Court decision called *Lone Wolf vs. Hitchcock*. The courts have required that treaty changes by Congress be specific and clearly intended. Treaties are not revoked or altered just because Congress passes a general law which in some cases would be opposed to treaty rights.

The reader is encouraged to consult the following sources for a more detailed discussion of treaty rights of Indian tribes:

Rennard Strickland and Charles F. Wilkinson, eds., *Felix S. Cohen's Handbook of Federal Indian Law: 1982 Edi-*

tion. (Michie, Bobbs-Merrill, Charlottesville, VA.,
1982)

Stephen L. Pevar, *The Rights of Indians and Tribes: The
Basic ACLU Guide to Indian and Tribal Rights.* 2nd
ed. (Southern Illinois University Press, Carbondale,
IL, 1992)

William C. Canby, *American Indian Law in a Nutshell.* 2nd
ed. (West Publishing Co., St. Paul, MN, 1988)

Charles F. Wilkinson, *American Indians, Time, and the Law:
Native Societies in a Modern Constitutional Democ-
racy* (Yale University Press, New Haven, CN 1987)

The courts have consistently held that Indian treaties are
binding agreements entered into by the federal government in return
for permanent land cessions. In these documents the federal government recognizes the limited sovereignty still held by American Indian
tribes, and the courts have set high tests to evaluate any attempts to
alter them.

Contents of This Volume

In the Name of the Salish & Kootenai Nation includes all of
the published primary documents relating to the Hell Gate Treaty that
are available in article form. It does not contain those sources which are
available as portions of books or as scattered references. The footnotes
will direct the reader in further study. The availability of the article by
Ignatius Burns, S.J., about Adrian Hoecken, S.J., including Hoecken's
letters has resulted in a disproportionate emphasis on Hoecken. Hoecken
did not play an active role in the treaty council but his letters do help
balance the government materials on the subject. It would be very valuable to have some sources from the Salish and Kootenai viewpoint, but
such sources are not now available. It would also have been helpful to
include a critical evaluation of the federal government's fulfillment of
the treaty provisions, but this material has not yet been pulled together.

The editors realize that this material has serious biases. We
are offering the collection because we believe the information is valuable despite the imbalance. Hopefully this publication will motivate
some of the young Salish and Kootenai scholars to do further research
about the treaty and its impact on the tribes.

In addition to a copy of the Hell Gate Treaty of 1855, this
book also contains reprints of three other works:

(1) Albert J. Partoll, "The Flathead Indian Treaty Council of 1855" *Pacific Northwest Quarterly,* volume 29, number 3 (July 1938) p. 283-314. We have used Partoll's notes from the 1938 edition, but have gone back to the original to include a correct transcription of the treaty council proceedings as recorded by James Doty, secretary for the treaty negotiations. The original transcript is now held by the Diplomatic Branch of the National Archives, Washington, D.C., and available in *Documents Relating to the Negotiations of Ratified and Unratified Treaties with Various Tribes of Indians, 1801-69,* National Archives Microfilm Publication T494, reel 5, frames 0834-0875. Albert Partoll, the editor of the 1938 edition was the author of a number of important studies of Western Montana history. A former student of Paul C. Phillips at the University of Montana in Missoula, Partoll served as the first editor of *Montana: The Magazine of Western History.* He died in Missoula in 1985.

(2) John C. Ewers, *Gustavus Sohon's Portraits of Flathead and Pend d'Oreille Indians, 1854,* Smithsonian Miscellaneous Collections, volume 110, number 7 (1948) p. 27-43, 47-54, 57-62, and 64-66. These portraits and biographical sketches of the Salish leadership in the 1850s provide a glimpse of some of the personalities involved in the treaty negotiations. John Ewers has long been recognized as one of the most knowledgeable students of Northern Plains Indians and his published books and papers over the years have been voluminous. He began the Plains Indian Museum in Browning and later spent much of his career doing research and writing while serving as a staff member of the Smithsonian Institution in Washington, D.C. Now retired, he is Senior Ethnologist Emeritus at the Smithsonian. In the 1940s while preparing these biographies, Ewers secured oral information about the individuals pictured from Pierre Pichette, the late Salish historian from Arlee, Montana, and from Martina Siwahsah and Baptiste Finley.

(3) Robert Ignatius Burns, S.J., "A Jesuit at the Hell Gate Treaty of 1855" *Mid-America,* volume 34, number 2 (April 1952) p. 87-103 and 197-114. Probably the most detailed analysis of the treaty negotiations yet published, Father Burn's paper also makes available for the first time important observations by Adrian Hoecken, S.J., an eye-witness to the council. Burns gathered much of this material while assistant archivist at the Oregon Province Archives at Gonzaga Univer-

6

sity in Spokane, Washington. This paper was included as a chapter in Burns' *The Jesuits and the Indian Wars of the Northwest* (Yale University Press, New Haven, Conn., 1966). The author is now professor at the University of California at Los Angeles.

Acknowledgements

We would like to thank Dr. John Ewers, the *Pacific Northwest Quarterly,* and *Mid-America* for permission to reprint these articles. The Oregon Province Archives, Gonzaga University, Spokane, Washington; the National Archives, Washington, D.C.; the National Anthropological Archives, Smithsonian Institution, Washington, D.C.; Washington State Historical Society, Tacoma, Washington; K. Ross Toole Archives, University of Montana, Missoula, Montana; and Montana Historical Society, Helena, kindly furnished illustrations. Marcia Bakry of the Department of Anthropology, Smithsonian Institution, drew the map of Western Montana.

We would like to express our appreciation to all those people at Salish Kootenai College who put up with us underfoot while we used their computers. This would especially include Roy BigCrane, Annette Brown, and Frank Tyro at the SKC Media Center and Joyce Silverthorne and David Broderick at the SKC Bilingual Program. For computer support, and for answering so many questions, there is no way we can adequately thank Al Anderson of the SKC Computer Department.

The editors would like to thank all who helped make this book possible and we hope it will contribute to increased understanding on the Flathead Reservation.

Robert Bigart
Clarence Woodcock

Pablo, Montana
June 1995

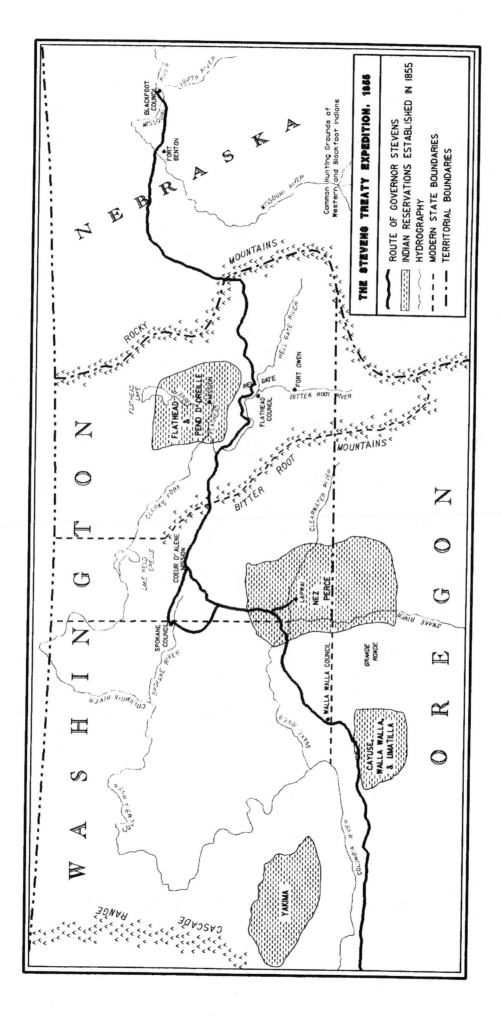

THE STEVENS TREATY EXPEDITION, 1855

ROUTE OF GOVERNOR STEVENS
INDIAN RESERVATIONS ESTABLISHED IN 1855
HYDROGRAPHY
MODERN STATE BOUNDARIES
TERRITORIAL BOUNDARIES

Common Hunting Grounds of
Western and Blackfoot Indians

NEBRASKA

WASHINGTON

OREGON

BLACKFOOT COUNCIL

FORT BENTON

MISSOURI RIVER

SOUTH RIVER

MISSOURI RIVER

MOUNTAINS

ROCKY

HELL GATE RIVER

FORT OWEN

HELL GATE

FLATHEAD COUNCIL

BITTER ROOT RIVER

FLATHEAD LAKE

FLATHEAD RESERVE

FLATHEAD, PEND D'OREILLE & MISSION

BITTER ROOT

MOUNTAINS

CLARKS FORK

CLEARWATER RIVER

COEUR D'ALENE MISSION

LAKE PEND OREILLE

LAPWAI

NEZ PERCE

SNAKE RIVER

SPOKANE COUNCIL

SPOKANE RIVER

COLUMBIA RIVER

WALLA WALLA COUNCIL

GRANDE RONDE

SNAKE RIVER

CAYUSE, WALLA WALLA & UMATILLA

COLUMBIA RIVER

COLUMBIA RIVER

YAKIMA

CASCADE RANGE

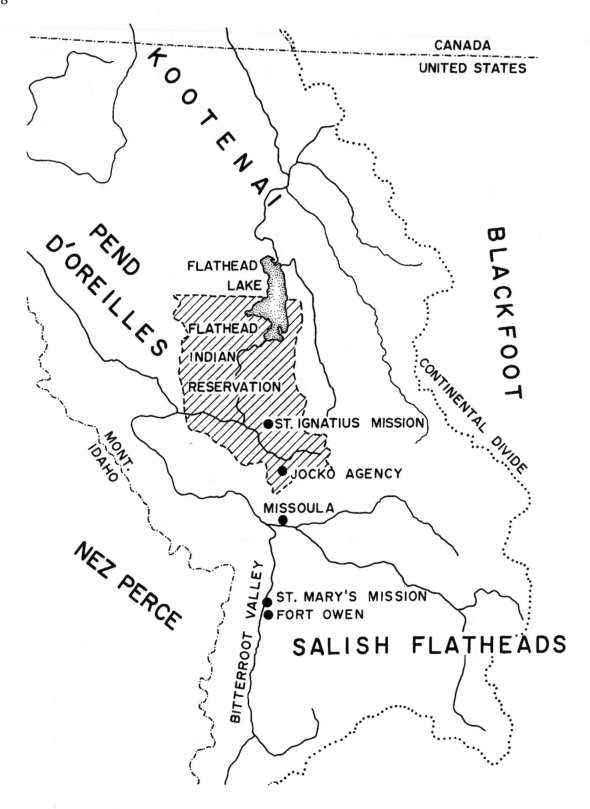

CANADA
UNITED STATES

KOOTENAI

PEND D'OREILLES

BLACKFOOT

FLATHEAD LAKE

FLATHEAD INDIAN RESERVATION

●ST. IGNATIUS MISSION

CONTINENTAL DIVIDE

MONT.
IDAHO

●JOCKO AGENCY

MISSOULA
●

NEZ PERCE

BITTERROOT VALLEY

●ST. MARY'S MISSION
●FORT OWEN

SALISH FLATHEADS

Tribes and Historical Locations of Western Montana

Treaty with the Flatheads, etc., 1855

Articles of agreement and convention made and concluded at the treaty-ground at Hell Gate, in the Bitter Root Valley, this sixteenth day of July, in the year one thousand eight hundred and fifty-five, by and between Isaac I. Stevens, governor and superintendent of Indian Affairs for the Territory of Washington, on the part of the United States, and the undersigned chiefs, head-men, and delegates of the confederated tribes of the Flathead, Kootenay, and Upper Pend d'Oreilles Indians, on behalf of and acting for said confederated tribes, and being duly authorized thereto by them. It being understood and agreed that the said confederated tribes do hereby constitute a nation, under the name of the Flathead Nation, with Victor, the head chief of the Flathead tribe, as the head chief of the said nation, and that the several chiefs, head-men, and delegates, whose names are signed to this treaty, do hereby, in behalf of their respective tribes, recognize Victor as said head chief.

July 16,1855
12 Stats., 975.
Ratified Mar.8,1859.
Proclaimed Apr. 18, 1859.

ARTICLE 1. The said confederated tribe of Indians hereby cede, relinquish, and convey to the United States all their right, title, and interest in and to the country occupied or claimed by them, bounded and described as follows, to wit:

Cession of lands to the United States.

From Charles J. Kappler, editor, *Indian Affairs: Laws and Treaties* (U.S. Government Printing Office, Washington, D.C., 1904) volume 2, p. 722-724.

Commencing on the main ridge of the Rocky Mountains at the forty-ninth (49th) parallel of latitude, thence westwardly on that parallel to the divide between the Flat-bow or Kootenay River and Clarke's Fork, thence southerly and southeasterly along said divide to the one hundred and fifteenth degree of longitude, (115°) thence in a southwesterly direction to the divide between the sources of the St. Regis Borgia and the Coeur d'Alene Rivers, thence southeasterly and southerly along the main ridge of the Bitter Root Mountains to the divide between the head-waters of the Koos-koos-kee River and of the southwestern fork of the Bitter Root River, thence easterly along the divide separating the waters of the several tributaries of the Bitter Root River from the waters flowing into the Salmon and Snake Rivers to the main ridge of the Rocky Mountains, and thence northerly along said main ridge to the place of beginning.

ARTICLE 2. There is, however, reserved from the lands above ceded, for the use and occupation of the said confederated tribes, and as a general Indian reservation, upon which may be placed other friendly tribes and bands of Indians of the Territory of Washington who may agree to be consolidated with the tribes parties to this treaty, under the common designation of the Flathead Nation, with Victor, head chief of the Flathead tribe, as the head chief of the nation, the tract of land included within the following boundaries, to wit:

Commencing at the source of the main branch of the Jocko River; thence along the divide separating the waters flowing into the Bitter Root River from those flowing into the Jocko to a point on Clarke's Fork between the Camash and Horse Prairies; thence northerly to, and along the divide bounding on the west the Flathead River, to a point due west from the point half way in latitude between the northern and southern extremities of the Flathead Lake; thence on a due east course to the divide whence the Crow, the Prune, the So-ni-el-em and the Jocko Rivers take their rise, and thence southerly along said divide to the place of beginning.

All which tract shall be set apart, and, so far as necessary, surveyed and marked out for the exclusive use and benefit of said confederated tribes as an Indian reservation. Nor shall any white man, excepting those in the employment of the Indian department, be permitted to reside upon the said reservation without permission of the confederated tribes, and the superintendent and agent. And the said confederated tribes agree to remove to and settle upon the same within one year after the ratification of this treaty. In the meantime it shall be lawful for them to reside upon any ground not in the actual claim and occupation of citizens of the United States, and upon any ground claimed or occupied, if with the permission of the owner or claimant.

Guaranteeing however the right to all citizens of the United States to enter upon and occupy as settlers any lands not actually occupied and cultivated by said Indians at this time, and not included in the reservation above named. *And provided,* That any substantial improvements heretofore made by any Indian, such as fields enclosed and cultivated and houses erected upon the lands hereby ceded, and which he may be compelled to abandon in consequence of this treaty, shall be valued under the direction of the President of the United States and payment made therefor in money or improvements of an equal value be made for said Indian upon the reservation; and no Indian will be required to abandon the improvements aforesaid, now occupied by him, until their value in money or improvements of an equal value shall be furnished him as aforesaid.

ARTICLE 3. *And provided,* That if necessary for the public convenience roads may be run through the said reservation, and, on the other hand, the right of way with free access from the same to the nearest public highway is secured to them, as also the right in common with citizens of the United States to travel upon all public highways.

Marginal notes:

Whites not to reside thereon unless, etc.

Indians to be allowed for improvements on land ceded.

Roads may be made through reservation.

Rights and privileges of Indians.

The exclusive right of taking fish in all the streams running through or bordering said reservation is further secured to said Indians; as also the right of taking fish at all usual and accustomed places, in common with citizens of the Territory, and of erecting temporary buildings for curing; together with the privilege of hunting, gathering roots and berries, and pasturing their horses and cattle upon open and unclaimed land.

Payments by the United States.

ARTICLE 4. In consideration of the above cession, the United States agree to pay to the said confederated tribes of Indians, in addition to the goods and provisions distributed to them at the time of signing this treaty the sum of one hundred and twenty thousand dollars, in the following manner—that is to say: For the first year after the ratification hereof, thirty-six thousand dollars, to be expended under the direction of the President, in providing for their removal to the reservation, breaking up and fencing farms, building houses for them, and for such other objects as he may deem necessary. For the next four years, six thousand dollars each year; for the next five years, five thousand dollars each year; for the next five years, four thousand dollars each year; and for the next five years, three thousand dollars each year.

How to be applied.

All which said sums of money shall be applied to the use and benefit of the said Indians, under the direction of the President of the United States, who may from time to time determine, at his discretion, upon what beneficial objects to expend the same for them, and the superintendent of Indian affairs, or other proper officer, shall each year inform the President of the wishes of the Indians in relation thereto.

United States to establish schools.

ARTICLE 5. The United States further agree to establish at suitable points within said reservation, within one year after the ratification hereof, an agricultural and industrial school, erecting the necessary buildings, keeping the same in repair, and providing it with furniture, books, and stationery, to be located at the agency, and to be free to the children of the said tribes, and to employ a suitable instructor or instructors. To furnish one blacksmith shop, to which shall be attached a tin and gun shop; one carpenter's shop; one wagon and plough-maker's shop; and to keep the same in repair, and furnished with the necessary tools. To employ two farmers, one blacksmith, one tinner, one gunsmith, one carpenter, one wagon and plough maker, for the instruction of the Indians in trades, and to assist them in the same. To erect one saw-mill and one flouring-mill, keeping the same in repair and furnished with the necessary tools and fixtures, and to employ two millers. To erect a hospital, keeping the same in repair, and provided with the necessary medicines and furniture, and to employ a physician; and to erect, keep in repair, and provide the necessary furniture the buildings required for the accommodation of said employees. The said buildings and establishments to be maintained and kept in repair as aforesaid, and the employees to be kept in service for the period of twenty years.

Mechanics' shop.

Hospital.

And in view of the fact that the head chiefs of the said confederated tribes of Indians are expected and will be called upon to perform many services of a public character, occupying much of their time, the United States further agree to pay to each of the Flathead, Kootenay, and Upper Pend d'Oreilles tribes five hundred dollars per year, for the term of twenty years after the ratification hereof, as a salary for such persons as the said confederated tribes may select to be their head chiefs, and to build for them at suitable points on the reservation a comfortable house, and properly furnish the same, and to plough and fence for each of them ten acres of land. The salary to be paid to, and the said houses to be occupied by, such head chiefs so long as they may be elected to that position by their tribes, and no longer.

To pay salary to head chiefs.

And all the expenditures and expenses contemplated in this article of this treaty shall be defrayed by the United States, and shall not be deducted from the annu-

Certain expenses to be borne by the United States and not charged on annuities.

ities agreed to be paid to said tribes. Nor shall the cost of transporting the goods for the annuity payments be a charge upon the annuities, but shall be defrayed by the United States.

Lots may be assigned to individuals.

ARTICLE 6. The President may from time to time, at his discretion, cause the whole, or such portion of such reservation as he may think proper, to be surveyed into lots, and assign the same to such individuals or families of the said confederated tribes as are willing to avail themselves of the privilege, and will locate on the same as a permanent home, on the same terms and subject to the same regulations as are provided in the sixth article of the treaty with the Omahas, so far as the same may be applicable.

Ante, p. 612.

Annuities not to pay individual debts.

ARTICLE 7. The annuities of the aforesaid confederated tribes of Indians shall not be taken to pay the debts of individuals.

Indians to preserve friendly relations.

ARTICLE 8. The aforesaid confederated tribes of Indians acknowledge their dependence upon the Government of the United States, and promise to be friendly with all citizens thereof, and pledge themselves to commit no depredations upon the property of such citizens. And should any one or more of them violate this pledge, and the fact be satisfactorily proved before the agent, the property taken shall be returned, or, in default thereof, or if injured or destroyed, compensation may be made by the Government out of the annuities. Nor will they make war on any other tribe except in self-defence, but will submit all matters of difference between them and other Indians to the Government of the United States, or its agent, for decision, and abide thereby. And if any of the said Indians commit any depredations on any other Indians within the jurisdiction of the United States, the same rule shall prevail as that prescribed in this article, in case of depredations against citizens. And the said tribes agree not to shelter or conceal offenders against the laws of the United States, but to deliver them up to the authorities for trial.

Indians to pay for depredations, not to make war except, etc.

To surrender offenders.

ARTICLE 9. The said confederated tribes desire to exclude from their reservation the use of ardent spirits, and to prevent their people from drinking the same; and therefore it is provided that any Indian belonging to said confederated tribes of Indians who is guilty of bringing liquor into said reservation, or who drinks liquor, may have his or her proportion of the annuities withheld from him or her for such time as the President may determine.

ARTICLE 10. The United States further agree to guaranty the exclusive use of the reservation provided for in this treaty, as against any claims which may be urged by the Hudson Bay Company under the provisions of the treaty between the United States and Great Britain of the fifteenth of June, eighteen hundred and forty-six, in consequence of the occupation of a trading-post on the Pru-in River by the servants of that company.

ARTICLE 11. It is, moreover, provided that the Bitter Root Valley, above the Loo-lo Fork, shall be carefully surveyed and examined, and if it shall prove, in the judgment of the President, to be better adapted to the wants of the Flathead tribe than the general reservation provided for in this treaty, then such portions of it as may be necessary shall be set apart as a separate reservation for the said tribe. No portion of the Bitter Root Valley, above the Loo-lo Fork, shall be opened to settlement until such examination is had and the decision of the President made known.

ARTICLE 12. This treaty shall be obligatory upon the contracting parties as soon as the same shall be ratified by the President and Senate of the United States.

In testimony whereof, the said Isaac I. Stevens, governor and superintendent of Indian affairs for the Territory of Washington, and the undersigned head chiefs, chiefs and principal men of the Flathead, Kootenay, and Upper Pend d'Oreilles tribes of Indians, have hereunto set their hands and seals, at the place and on the day and year herein-before written.

Annuities to be reserved from those who drink, etc., ardent spirits.

Guarantee of reservation against certain claims of Hudson Bay Company.

Bitter Root Valley to be surveyed, and portions may be set apart for reservation.

Meanwhile not to be opened for settlement.

When treaty to take effect.

Isaac I. Stevens, [L. S.]
Governor and Superintendent Indian Affairs W. T.

Victor, head chief of the Flathead Nation,
    his x mark.   [L.S.]
Alexander, chief of the Upper Pend d'Oreilles,
    his x mark.   [L.S.]
Michelle, chief of the Kootenays,
    his x mark.   [L.S.]
Ambrose, his x mark.   [L.S.]
Pah-soh, his x mark.   [L.S.]
Bear Track, his x mark.   [L.S.]
Adolphe, his x mark.   [L.S.]
Thunder, his x mark.   [L.S.]
Big Canoe, his x mark.   [L.S.]
Kootel Chah, his x mark.   [L.S.]
Paul, his x mark.   [L.S.]
Andrew, his x mark.   [L.S.]
Michelle, his x mark.   [L.S.]
Battiste, his x mark.   [L.S.]

Kootenays.

Gun Flint, his x mark.   [L.S.]
Little Michelle, his x mark.   [L.S.]
Paul See, his x mark.   [L.S.]
Moses. his x mark.   [L.S.]

James Doty, secretary
R. H. Lansdale, Indian Agent
W. H. Tappan, sub Indian Agent.
Henry R. Crosire,
Gustavus Sohon, Flathead Interpreter.
A. J. Hoecken, sp. mis.
William Craig.

1.

Articles of Agreement and Convention made and concluded at the Treaty Ground at Hell Gate, in the Bitter Root Valley this Sixteenth day of July in the year One thousand Eight hundred and fifty five, by and between Isaac I. Stevens, Governor and Superintendent of Indian Affairs for the Territory of Washington on the part of the United States, and the undersigned Chiefs, Head Men and Delegates of the Confederated Tribes of the Flat Head, Kootenay, and Upper Pend Oreilles Indians on behalf of and acting for said Confederated Tribes, and being duly authorized thereto by them.

It being understood and agreed that the said Confederated Tribes do hereby constitute a Nation under the name of the Flat Head Nation, with Victor the Head Chief of the Flat Head Tribe as the Head Chief of the said Nation, and that the several Chiefs, Head Men and Delegates whose names are signed to this Treaty, do hereby, in behalf of their respective Tribes, recognize Victor as said Head Chief.

Article 1.   The said Confederated Tribes of Indians hereby Cede relinquish and convey to the United States all their right, title and interest in and to the country occupied or claimed by them;

The first page of the original Hell Gate Treaty in the U.S. National Archives.

The signatures from original Hell Gate Treaty in U.S. National Archives.

Official Proceedings of the Hell Gate Treaty Council

notes by Albert J. Partoll

In 1855 Governor Isaac I. Stevens of Washington Territory negotiated the treaty between the United States and the Flathead Indian nation, consisting of the Flatheads or Selish proper, the Upper Pend d'Oreilles or Kalispells, and the Kootenay Indians. It was one of a series[1] of treaties concluded by Governor Stevens in 1854 and 1855, as superintendent of Indian affairs for Washington Territory, and was in accordance with his instructions to extinguish Indian sovereignty along the routes and territory of the explorations and surveys for a railroad route to the Pacific Ocean, under his direction in 1853 and 1854.

The treaty was anticipated by the Flathead nation as the beginning of a new era in their tribal history, since by it these Indians were to be assured protection against the inroads of the Blackfeet, their traditional foes, and to live at peace with them. Governor Stevens in his instructions of September 8, 1853, to Lieutenant John Mullan to visit the Flathead hunting camp on the Muscle Shell River and bring the chiefs to St. Mary's Village in the Bitter Root Valley for conference stated in part: "But the great duty which I place in your hands, is to carry from me a message of the Great Father to the Flatheads. Assure them that the Great Father appreciates their services and understands their merits; that he will hereafter protect them from the incursions of the Blackfeet, and other Indians east of the mountains, and make them live as friends; that he will send to them each year, certain articles which they most need; and that a faithful and intelligent agent shall live among them."[2]......

The official proceedings of this treaty council as recorded by James Doty, secretary of treaties of Washington Territory, are reproduced here with editorial notes and annotations, together with a letter by Governor Stevens relating to the treaty and explaining the decision of Victor. The manuscript and the appended letter are in the files of the National Archives, Washington, D. C.

ALBERT J. PARTOLL, Missoula, Montana

****

1. Hazard Stevens, *The Life of Isaac Ingalls Stevens* (Boston, 1900), II, 81-91 reviews these treaties; Charles J. Kappler, ed., *Indian Affairs: Laws and Treaties* (Washington, 1904), II, 722-725, gives them in detail. (*Senate Document* 58 Cong., 2 Sess., no 319, ser. 4624).

2. Isaac I. Stevens, "Report of Explorations for a Route for the Pacific Railroad . . . from St. Paul to Puget Sound," *Reports of Explorations and Surveys, . . .from the Mississippi River to the Pacific Ocean* (Washington, 1855), I, 34-35. (*Senate Executive Document* 33 Cong., 2 Sess., no. 78, ser. 758).

The notes are from Albert J. Partoll, editor, "The Flathead Indian Treaty Council of 1855" *Pacific Northwest Quarterly*, volume 29, number 3 (July 1938) p. 283-314. The text of the negotiations has been copied from the microfilm of the original in the National Archives available on reel 5 frames 0834 through 0875 of National Archives microfilm publication T494, *Documents Relating to the Negotiations of Ratified and Unratified Treaties with Various Tribes of Indians, 1801-69*. A number of mistakes and omissions in the 1938 version have been corrected. The present edition has standardized some of the spelling, added some punctuation and highlighted the names of speakers to facilitate use of the document. Brackets indicate editorial additions. Parenthetical insertions are in the original document.–**Bigart and Woodcock**.

Official Proceedings at the Council held by Governor Isaac I. Stevens, Supt. Indian Affairs, W. T., with the Flathead,[3] Pend Oreilles[4] and Kootenay Tribes of Indians at Hell Gate in the Bitter Root Valley, Washington Territory, commencing on the seventh day of July, 1855.

July 7th. Gov. Stevens[5] accompanied by various officers of the Indian Department reached the Indian camp near Hell Gate and was welcomed by all the Chiefs and Warriors of the Flathead, Kootenay and Pend Oreille Indians who rode out to meet the Governor's party.

The Governor selected for his camp and a council[6] ground a point on the Bitter Root River one mile from the Indian camp.

In the afternoon Victor,[7] Chief of the Flatheads, Alexander[8] of the Upper Pend Oreilles, and Michelle[9] of the Kootenays accompanied by a number of the principal men of the Tribes visited Governor Stevens at the Council Ground. After they had smoked[10] as usual upon such

3. The Flatheads here mentioned did not deform their heads, they are sometimes confused with coast tribes which did so. "Selish" or "Saylish" was their name for themselves.

4. The Upper Pend d'Oreilles or Kalispells. The spelling as it appears in the document is followed.

5. His biography is written by his son, Hazard Stevens, who was with his father in treaty negotiations.

6. This location has been known since as Council Grove. It is located six miles west of Missoula, Montana, near the north bank of the Clarks Fork River.

7. Victor was a noted chief and is mentioned in many early writings. He is mentioned frequently by Pierre-Jean De Smet: Hiram M. Chittenden and Alfred T. Richardson, eds., *Life, Letters and Travels of Father Pierre-Jean De Smet, S. J. 1801-1873* (New York, 1905). He was sometimes confused with another chief, Victor of the Lower Pend d'Oreilles. Victor of the Flatheads attended the Blackfoot council a few weeks later and signed the treaty. He died when about eighty on July 14, 1870.

8. Albert J. Partoll, ed., "The Blackfoot Indian Peace Council," *Frontier and Midland* (Missoula, Montana, Spring, 1937), XVII, 199-207. Alexander was head chief of the Kalispells and an ardent advocate of peaceful relations with the Blackfeet. He later signed the treaty with them, and made several speeches at their council.

9. He attended the Blackfoot council and is listed as a signer. He was an associate of Victor and Alexander, hunting and fighting their enemies with them.

10. To smoke with a man was a sign of friendly intent. Refusal to do so was a declaration of hostility or the belief that the other was not a friend.

occasions, of the tobacco given them, Gov. Stevens spoke to Victor as follows:

"You have heard I suppose of the Council at Walla Walla[11] and what was there said to the Indians. The treaties made there were fully explained. We made treaties with the Nez Perces and others, numbering in all some 6000 Indians, and placed them on reservations. I wish to make with you treaties similar to those made at that place, and on Monday I will speak to you about it and explain all things fully; but in the meantime the Flatheads and Nez Perces who came up with us were present at that council and can tell you all about it.

"The business here being concluded, I shall push on to Fort Benton to collect the Blackfeet for a council. We expect many of the Nez Perces here in a few days in charge of an Agent and Interpreter to meet you and go with you to the council near Fort Benton, where we expect to make a treaty which will keep the Blackfeet out of this valley, and if that will not do it we will then have soldiers who will. Some of the Blackfeet, the Great Chiefs you know are good and will listen to us. A commissioner is coming up the Missouri to meet me. The Great Father, the President, has directed us to make a treaty and he will see it carried out, and we hope it will forever settle your troubles with the Blackfeet. I saw you two years[12] ago and told you I would come to make a treaty, I hoped the next year. Two years have passed, but in the meantime, as you know, we have done all we could. Lt. Mullan,[13] Mr. Adams, Mr. Doty[14] these two you see here now, were left among the Indians to promote peace and we are determined to push this matter through.

"On Monday then at 10 o'clock I will talk with you here and explain everything."

Victor said: "The Blackfeet have troubled us very much."

Gov. Stevens: "I have heard of your troubles before and have done all I could to get this matter arranged at this time."

11. Lawrence Kip, *The Indian Council in the Valley of the Walla Walla, 1855* (San Francisco, 1855). Treaty with the Nez Perces and other Indians.

12. In the Bitter Root Valley on September 30 and October 1, 1853. Governor Stevens discussed the matter of future negotiations of treaty.

13. Lieutenant John Mullan, later promoted to rank of captain, after whom the Mullan Military road was named and author of *Report on the Construction of a Military Road* . . . (Washington, 1863) and *Miners and Travelers' Guide* . . . (New York, 1865).

14. James Doty was secretary of treaties. His assistance was invaluable in bringing the Blackfeet to treaty.

Victor: "I am going to tell what has happened since you were here. Twelve men have been killed when out hunting—not on war parties. I fear the whites and kept quiet. I cannot tell how many horses have been stolen since.

"Now I listen and hear what you wish me to do. Were it not for you I would have had my revenge ere this. They (the Blackfeet) have stolen horses seven times this spring."

July 9th, Monday.

The Indians began to assemble at 1/2 past 12 o'clock and at 1/2 past 1 p.m. the Council opened.

Present: Officers of the Council.

Gov. I. I. Stevens, Supt. Indian Affairs and Commissioner holding treaties.

James Doty, Secretary.

H. R. Crosbie,[15] Commissary and Clerk.

Thomas Adams,[16] Special Indian Agent for Flathead, Pend Oreilles & Kootenays.

R. H. Lansdale,[17] Agent Indians Washington Territory.

G. Sohon[18]   )

) Interpreters.

Benj. Kiser[19])

15. Hubert H. Bancroft, *History of the Pacific States of North America: Washington, Idaho, and Montana, 1845-1889* (San Francisco, 1890), XXVI, 73, 98. H. R. Crosbie, a member of the Stevens treaty party, who was in the first territorial legislature of Washington of 1853. He signed the treaty here being arranged for. Kappler, *Indian Treaties,* has a misprint of his name giving it as "Crosier," and Stevens, *Stevens,* gives his name as "Crosby."

16. Thomas Adams, assistant artist of the Stevens explorations, was appointed special Indian agent in 1854. He remained in the Bitter Root Valley and vicinity until 1864 when he left for the east. In 1866, he was farming in Maryland.

17. Dr. R. H. Lansdale was appointed Indian agent for the Flatheads in 1855, and was succeeded shortly after by John Owen. He signed the treaty here being made.

18. Gustavus Sohon served with the Stevens exploration expedition of 1853 and 1854, and also with the Mullan road building enterprise of 1859-1862. He is spoken of as topographer and map maker, and he was also an artist of note. Mullan used his illustrations in his book on the construction of the road.

19. Frank H. Woody, "A Sketch of the Early History of Western Montana," *Contributions to the Historical Society of Montana* . . . (Helena, Montana, 1896), II, 93. A half-breed Shawnee who could speak English and was reliable as an interpreter. He also was interpreter at the Blackfoot treaty for the Flatheads. In later years he was a trader and rancher in western Montana. Sometimes his name is given as "Keiser."

Tobacco was distributed, and after the usual time spent in smoking, Gov. Stevens addressed the Indians as follows:

"My Children: I am glad to see so many of you here today. I have come to fulfill a promise which I made you two years since. I have come to make a treaty with you if we can agree upon the terms. I have already made treaties with the Nez Perces and with other tribes: several Flatheads were present at those treaties; they have told you about them. I wish to make with you a treaty similar to the treaty I made with the Nez Perces.

"There are here present three tribes, the Flatheads under their chief Victor; the Upper Pend Oreilles under their chief Alexander; the Kootenays under their chief Michelle. I am sorry that the Lower Pend Oreilles with their chief Victor[20] are not here.

"I wish to make a treaty with the Flatheads, Upper and Lower Pend Oreilles and Kootenays all as one nation. We wish you four tribes to sell your land to the Great Father and live on one tract of land; that tract of land to be large enough for your cattle and farms. The climate of the tract to be mild enough for your animals to graze in winter.

"In the treaty[21] besides providing for your having a tract of land for your homes, you will have the privilege of going on to the land you have sold to get roots and berries and to kill game except where the land is actually occupied by a white settler.

"For this sale of your land we propose to make certain payments which I will now explain. An Agent will live amongst you. You have already had an agent, Mr. Adams, but he has not had the means to do much with; he has not received much from the Great Father; he has done all he could, his words have gone to the Great Father, and the Great Father says you shall be cared for.

"You will have a school, a good school amongst you; at this school your children will learn to read and write, and they will learn trades such as desire it. You will have a hospital and a physician for the care of your sick. You will have a farmer, you will have a blacksmith with tools, you will have a wheelwright, a man to make wagons and plows; you will have a saw mill and a grist mill.

20. Victor of the Lower Pend d'Oreilles is sometimes mistaken for Victor of the Flatheads.
21. Kappler, *Indian Treaties,* 722-725, has the text of the treaty.

"The school, the farmer, the blacksmith, the wheelwright and the saw and grist mills you will have for twenty years; then you can take care of yourselves. This will be one part of the payment; the other part I will now explain. You will be supplied with means to start your farms, and to give you clothing, tools and cooking utensils and something in the way of houses. It will be enough to clothe every person, and to give every one cooking utensils and farming tools enough to start with. Then each year for twenty years we shall make additions to what we gave at first. You will be expected to live on the same good terms with each other as you have been living. I need not say a word about that. You will be expected to live on good terms with all friendly tribes. We will soon go over to the Blackfoot country, then if a treaty be made, and they prove friendly, you will of course live on good terms with them. When we get to the Blackfoot country we will talk about it. The Great Father is determined that you shall be safe on the reservation from the attacks of the Blackfeet;—this I will say to the Blackfeet in Council, you being present. I believe we can make peace, but enough of that, I will reserve that for the Blackfeet Council.

"On another point I wish to speak plainly;—within yourselves you will be governed by your own laws. The agent will see that you are not interfered with, but will support the authority of the chiefs. You will respect the laws which govern the white man and the white man will respect your laws. We look with favor on the missionaries[22] that come amongst the Indians where they desire them and I think their coming may do them good. The priest will be your friend, but he will *not* have no [sic] control whatever over your affairs. The priest will advise you in your spiritual affairs—that which relates to God, but he will have no control over your temporal affairs, your own laws; that you will manage yourselves.

"I think you understand the different points of the treaties. All your tribes, Flatheads, Upper and Lower Pend Oreilles and Kootenays to live on one reservation. That reservation to be large enough for all your animals and farms; and the rest of the land to be the Great Father's for his white children, you in addition to have the privilege to kill game, pasture your animals, dig roots and gather berries upon lands not

22. See reference, footnote 24, and Indian regard for.

Isaac Ingalls Stevens

(1818-1862)

The subtitle of the most recent biography of Isaac Stevens characterized him as a "Young Man in a Hurry." Stevens' ambition and temperment are important in understanding his attitude in negotiating the Hell Gate Treaty of 1855. He obviously had greater dreams than just being Governor of Washington Territory, and he was not about to allow the worries of a group of "parochial" chiefs undermine his personal goals.

Born and raised in New England in an established Puritan family of modest means, Stevens won an appointment to West Point and graduated at the head of his class in 1839. After graduation Stevens received a commission in the prestigous Army Corps of Engineers. He supervised construction of various East Coast forts until 1847 when he saw action in the Mexican-American War. After the war he wrote a book about his wartime experiences and worked on the United States Coast Survey of the east coast.

In 1853 he secured the appointment as Governor of Washington Territory which then included Western Montana. He was also made leader of the survey for the northern route for a transcontinental railroad. Part of the railroad work involved surveying the mountain passes and geography of Western Montana. The results of his work were published in a three volume report appearing in 1855 and 1860.

Stevens first met the Salish and Kootenai Indians during his railroad survey. He tried to conclude a peace treaty between the Rocky Mountain tribes and the Blackfeet on the Plains. As territorial governor, Stevens was automatically Superintendent of Indian Affairs for the territory. In 1854 and 1855 he conducted a series of treaty councils with the Indian tribes in Washington in order to extinguish Indian title to the land and open it to increased white settlement. First he negotiated several treaties with tribes west of the Cascades, and in the summer of 1855 he dealt with the Central Washington tribes in the Walla Walla council and the Eastern Washington (or Western Montana) tribes in the Hell Gate council. After completing these land cession treaties, he met in the Judith River country to arrange a treaty of peace between the Blackfeet and the Rocky

Mountain tribes, including the Salish and Kootenai. The peace treaty was signed but was effective for only a short time.

Many years of friction between Indians and whites were aggravated by the land cession treaties; later in 1855 war broke out between the whites and some of the tribes of the Walla Walla council. Other disturbances developed west of the Cascades and the resultant Indian-white war threatened Stevens' elaborate plans to settle the Indian land claims in Washington Territory. Stevens' use of martial law during the war and his general Indian policies came under public attack. The attacks caused Congress to delay approval of the treaties until 1859.

Stevens was elected as the Washington Territorial Delegate to Congress from 1857 to 1861. During this period he secured appropriations for the Mullan Road and lobbied successfully for approval of the treaties.

With the outbreak of the Civil War in 1861, he rejoined the Union Army as a colonel. He took part in several campaigns on the eastern front, and secured the rank of Brigadier General before being killed at Chantilly, Virginia, on September 1, 1862.

For further information about Stevens see the excellent biography by Kent D. Richards, *Isaac I. Stevens: Young Man in a Hurry* (Brigham Young University Press, Provo, UT, 1979)–**Bigart and Woodcock.**

occupied by white settlers—your payment to consist in schools and farms and mills and shops and a physician for 20 years.

"The first year a large amount of clothing, of cooking utensils and everything to start your farms and you will have an addition of the same things every year for twenty years.

"Will such a treaty suit you? If it will suit you then we have to agree where the reservation shall be and what the amount of these things shall be. I wish now the chiefs to tell me whether they are pleased with this kind of a treaty. I wish now to hear from them."

Victor (Flathead Chief) said: "I am very tired now and my people. You (the Governor) are the only man who has offered to aid us. I have not been able to do anything for my people. If my young men could see they might be afraid; they do not understand how the whites punish. I am very glad to see you, and that you have come to my place. My country is very small. I think God is willing that we should have a small piece of ground—my country is very bad; that is all the way I can talk.

"I have two places,[23] here is mine (Bitter Root Valley) and yonder across the mts. (Flathead river) is mine. I will think of it and tell you which is the best. I believe you wish to assist me to help my children here so that they may have plenty to eat, so that they may save their souls.

"There is very little land here: I cannot offer you a large piece. I have only a small piece: that is all I have to say."

Alexander (Pend Oreille Chief) said: "You know you have a white skin. I am poor; I am an Indian. I cannot look around me. I think my country is good. I think I am doing right, and now you come to my place you white man—now you talk to me—you tell me it is not good, how you are doing, this is good. We have a God Almighty; we were not made for nothing. We have a place to be punished. You say you do not like these bad things. The white man told me God Almighty did not like bad things, and when I heard that I think that I was very glad that I have to do so and so, this way is very good, take this good road—now I talking my people are sitting around me. You see my position my children—they never hear. I like all my children. You are talking to me now my big Father. You have told me you have to make your own laws to punish your

23. Since the Bitter Root Valley was more sheltered and farther from the inroads of the Blackfeet, Victor did not want to move, nor did he believe it to be sufficiently large for the consolidation of the three tribes there. These facts will be brought out as the council progresses.

children. I like my children. I think I could not head them to make them go straight. I think it is with you to do so. If I take your own way, your law, my people then will be frightened. These growing people are all the same—perhaps those who come after them may see it well before them. I do not know your laws, perhaps if we see a rope, if we see how it punishes we will be frightened. When they (the priests) talked to them, tried to teach them, they all left him. I am very glad to see the white men.

"My children—may be when the whites instruct you, you may see it before you. Now this is my ground—we are poor, we Indians. The priest is settled over there[24] (pointing across the mountain); there where he is I am very well satisfied. The priest instructs me and this people here. I am very well content with the priest and am very well satisfied with you. I will talk hereafter about the ground—I am done for today."

Red Wolf[25] (Flathead) said: "We gathered up yesterday— these people you see here. Here are the three nations that spoke; they think they are three nations. I think it was this way yesterday. Here is the ground I was talking about yesterday. I think myself there are three tribes here—they have their own places—they think they own my ground. I thought these three nations were going to talk, each about their own lands. Now I hear the governor and hear him talking. My ground is all cut up in pieces; a while ago you spoke. What I made my mind up to yesterday perhaps it will be that way now. They are not three nations— they are only one perhaps. They did not talk about their own lands yesterday. I think it is so. I do not (think?) it is right to talk about this land. By and by when we go back to the camp we will talk about it— perhaps tomorrow. We will talk it over tonight or tomorrow how much land we have; then you will know. If we can agree then we will talk it over here. I think this is my ground. I think of the three nations this belongs to the Flatheads—this is closed up by mountains. There is another place over yonder—across the mountains—that belongs to the Pend Oreilles. I do not know where the country of the Kootenays is. It is a long distance off. I made up my mind yesterday. I believe we did not agree. I thought

24. St. Ignatius Mission was founded in 1854 in the Flathead Valley. See reference, footnote 39.
25. Stevens, *Stevens,* II, 82, lists him as Red Wing, but this is obviously a mistake. Red Wolf was also known as Esac and Isaac. His mother was a Flathead and his father a Kootenay. See reference, footnote 44. Stevens has several extracts from the proceedings in his book.

we had two places this ground the Flatheads—that across the mountains the Pend Oreilles—perhaps not, perhaps we are all one—this is the reason I speak in this manner. I am very poor. We made up another mind yesterday—today it is different, we did not come to an end in council. We will go back and have another council. The others who think differently will talk about it."

Gov. Stevens said: "My children—The words of Esac who has spoken last are good. It will be well for you to talk the matter over in your camp, and then tomorrow we will meet again. I will say one word in reference to placing you all on one reservation. I think we can do more for you in that way—the agent can see the treaty is carried; your school will be better; your sick will be better cared for by the physician. Think the matter over well. I made two [three] treaties [at Walla Walla] before I came here. In one treaty three different tribes were put together; in the other treaty four different tribes were put together. We made a third treaty with the Nez Perces, a large tribe numbering more than all of you—we made the treaty with them alone. If you have two tracts, as the agent and physician can only live on one tract, those of the other tract cannot be as well cared for. Your living on one reservation will not make any difference with regard to things that you very much value now. Those who want a priest can have one, we do not propose to say to you, you shall have a priest or you shall not have a priest; that is a matter of your free choice. We promise you an agent that will see what you agree to and we agree to is carried out. Now we wish you to go to your own camp; talk the matter over amongst yourselves, we will meet in the morning, a little earlier than we have done today."

The council then adjourned at 4 p.m.

———————————

July 10th, Tuesday.

The Indians assembled at 2 p.m. and at 2 1/2 p.m. the council opened.

Present the same as yesterday.

Governor Stevens said: "My children: I explained yesterday the kind of a treaty I wished to make with you; that I desired the four tribes—the Flatheads, The Upper and Lower Pend 'Oreilles and Kootenays to go on one tract of land. You went to your camp and have since been thinking and talking about it: you have come here; I wish to know what you think about it. Speak out your minds fully."

Big Canoe[26] (Pend 'Oreille) said: "Listen I will speak. I spoke a while ago—I heard—I talked, then I went away, now you see all these people. I will not go away now. Some of them said 'It is good for you to go' that is the reason I come here; that is the way I spoke—I am going to tell you what I heard when I went away. I said to them perhaps you are mad; I am very glad of it—then I left. I spoke to them in this way. It appears to me you have two ways—how is it? When you talk you tremble, ashamed of yourself, are you afraid of him? (the Gov.) We are not talking bad—we are counseling—he is a very smart chief. You do not know what to do ? If you (Victor) had told me before, I would have spoken long ago about this our land. Now I told him (Victor) when I do talk I will tell you what we will do with this, our rights. It is our land—when I first saw you, you white man, when you were travelling through, I would not tell you take this piece it is our land—when you come to see me I believe you will help me. If you make a farm I would not go there and pull up your crops. I would not drive you away—farm it—it is our land both of us. If I go to your place on your land—If I get there [and say] give me a little piece. I wonder would you say here take it. I will wait till you give it. I will be amongst you, very good, I am with you. It is just like my own country—then I would come back to my own country. That is the way with you white man. I expect that is the same way you want me to do here, this place. You want to settle here me with you.

"Here you are going back and forth on our land: go back to your country—we [are] all one—we [are] all one close together. We [are] all great friends you white man. When my old people long ago first saw you we were friends—we never spilt the blood of one of you. They my old people are gone, all of them—it is the same now, I am the same, I never saw your blood. I want my place. I always thought no one wanted ever to talk about my place. Now you talk, you white man—now I have heard. I wish the whites to stop coming. You know everything you white man—

26. Frederick W. Hodge, ed., "Handbook of American Indians North of Mexico," *Bureau of American Ethnology, Bulletin 30* (Washington, 1907), Part 1, 146. Big Canoe signed the treaty with the Blackfeet in October, 1855. He was a firm friend of the whites and a leader against his Blackfoot enemies. He was born about 1799 and died in western Montana in 1882. His talk appears to have suffered in places from translation or recording.

you come and talk about my country, then you would say we are very poor. You just talk as you please to us; it is that way. Now you tell me never to go to war. Then I sit [sat] down, I kept quiet—I was listening to you and you wanted to talk—now [that] you are here I think [it is] so, I wish it may be good—perhaps you will put me in a trap, if I do not listen to you, you chiefs, white men—I will beg you, I told this when you talk my chief (Victor) you tremble this way, I wouldn't speak, I wouldn't tremble, he is a chief—we all are people—you are white—I am black. I know you, you, you my chiefs. My heart is heavy because you could not make it up yesterday. I am very poor, we heard you long ago. I hope it is so.

"When I lay [lie] down my heart is sad, now my chief you say now I am blind if I want to talk. Here are my eyes, my heart, my brain, I study. You white men; there are your eyes[27] lying all over the table, that is the reason you are smart, you always look at your papers; now you talk, it is right when you talk straight. I from my heart and my brains speak. I told my chiefs that when I think I believe I am going to talk this way; the way I beg you—when we call for some of our things I expect you want it then your Indian children. When you see something you say give it to me, I like it. You speaking and I tell you no—I think yes, don't impose upon us. I think yes you like it. Let us alone now. You tell us give us your land; if we say no, I am very poor, that is all the small piece I have got. That is the reason I have come, I am not going to let it go I did not come to make trouble. Therefore I would say I am very poor.

"You Flatheads I think this is my country, I don't think I made a mistake, my grand father's country. I was raised up there across the mountains. I saw my aunt over there, she tells me I am pure Pend 'Oreille. I think I have two bodies; this is mine too, that is the reason I talk; we are talking bad [to] one another, I beg you. I told these people a while ago, now you give me a piece of your land. He is a chief, if we tell him we are very poor, he will keep us—no perhaps he thinks yes we are very poor, he likes my country, we are very poor, we do not like to impose upon each other, this is what I am talking about. When we ask further

27. Refers to papers, notes, and memoranda. It must be remembered that the Indians were handicapped in that they did not have the facilities, training or experience of the whites. They had to rely upon interpreters to present their case, hence the interpretations as here recorded may at times be their spoken words and also their interpolations in the sign language.

little things, then you will think we won't give you any land. You will stop anyhow both sides. Talk about treaty,[28] where did I kill you? when did you kill me? What is the reason we are talking about treaties; that is what I said, we are friends, you are not my enemy. I said to them you do not know what to do. I expect you thought so when you tell the Governor. No, I expect you will stop powder[29] and ball being given us. Why would he stop it. When did I shoot you with your own powder and ball. Our old people when they saw you knew what powder and ball was and never tried to frighten a white man with it; here are the last of us— you see them all now sitting around, where have we made a difficulty with the whites. Here is my country, I think it is in a good place, not a dangerous place. You white man don't be afraid, you can see it—the Blackfeet, your own powder and ball shooting at us and you white man. Now I and you, you white man, both die with your own powder and ball. I think so when I think about it—stop that, quit giving them powder and ball.

"What will you do with us, we are very poor, you see us sitting around here, you know it yourself, we do not ramble about on war parties. There is a Frenchman (Indian name for all traders) coming. I will [not] hide where no one can see me and kill him. No; when I see a white man I go up to him; it makes me smile, I shake hands with him; that is the reason I ought to be let alone. You white people are smart and all the time teaching me. I don't want you to impose upon me. I want you to stop. I am that way you white man like yourself. I am glad to see you—I don't [want] you white man to be sorry for it and you my people. I did not think you white people would tell all over the country about me. You will never see in your papers that the Flatheads or Pend 'Oreilles have killed any of you—perhaps you are glad of it—I am proud of my old people—I am very poor—they had only a bow and arrow when they saw their enemies; they fought them a long while and then left them—then they say [from] you white man, from you we got guns and powder, that is the reason my

28. The Indians regarded a treaty as an agreement for friendly relationship generally after a disturbance, battle, or injury. They had always professed friendship for the whites, hence were somewhat at a loss to understand why the whites should advocate a complex and detailed treaty. They had previously understood that a treaty with the whites was to be of the nature of an alliance.

29. Traders sometimes adopted a policy of supplying firearms and accessories only to friendly tribes. Hostile Indians were at times deprived of these lest they become too bold. The strength of the Indians depended largely upon their equipment.

people have never spilt your blood. You see us, we are very few, our enemies are very afraid of us, we drove them before us. When my enemies charge upon you (trappers) here I am behind with your powder and ball, that is the reason we are fast friends. When I travel over the mountains towards my enemies I always think of you white men. I always thought the white man would help me, load my gun for me. Look at me how poor I am—look yonder at our enemies, you see it yourself—you white men with your own eyes. There is the priest, he says he thinks they will listen, here is me, I think they will not. I think if my children die it is all the same as white men—that is the way my heart and brain thinks.

"These are dark Indians, the bad fire (hell) comes to them, fighting one another; it is growing; they are getting worse and worse, there he lays, the Indian he takes some little things and puts on him, he let it go out—here you I sell it there where he lost his things this Indian, there where he put it out, there where they all raise up from one; their dark skins were ahed [*sic*] of them all—that is what I said a while ago. There you are carrying your things about. I won't hide what I said. I said I will ask him—is that the thing you put the fire out with, I will take it, I will never ask for it; then he said he did not know what to do—I cannot step over your things. There are your goods—which way shall I go. If I go to war I will take my horses. I am alone that is the way I studied. Suppose the Blackfeet come along—when he gets along side that things he cannot cross over—from there it will be white ground—both sides— I think so—

"Sometimes my people get mad when the Blackfeet kill us. There are you white men—you are just listening if they are plenty, you stop our people right here and prevent them going on war parties. We listen to the white people here on our ground—we are not afraid of our enemies, no, we are not afraid of them—that is the way with my heart. I don't know what these sitting around think about it. I don't know how they studied when the white men taught me how to pray. I don't know anything about it, though I spoke about it. The priest told me not to be running around in the lodges in the night, the way I saw myself, I did not like it, we came very near all night—the Crows came to us, then the Blackfeet—there is where it was lost. When I meet you I feel glad, when I got the news the white man, the chief, is coming, I was glad—Yonder are the Crows—then the Blackfeet, I don't want to see them.

Flathead Lake, Looking Southward

36

Mode of crossing rivers by the Flatheads and other Indians.

"Look at these Kootenays, I don't understand them; when I see the sun very low I pray—look at the Kootenays, they are always praying. Look at the Blackfeet, I don't like them. That is the way I talk to you sitting there, I am begging now—I am not talking saucy. Here are your goods—I am on one side and the Blackfeet on the other. If he steps over these goods and comes to me what would you think. I am only one side—I listen to you; he kills me, kills me all the time and drives my horses away, you know it, we are poor. We drove one band of horses from the Blackfeet[30]—I talked about it to my Indians. I said give me the horses back, my children—don't you know their pasture, let me have them— my chief took them back. You talked about it strong my father—I am afraid of your arms, way yonder from the Crows they took me—we talked about it, my chief took them back, that is the way we act.

"If I beg you I want you to help me: now you have just come here, now you are going over there and going to talk again. I do not know your minds—you are taking a great many goods, I think so; that is the reason I am quiet and sit down on my land. I thought nobody would talk about land, would trouble me. Look at them sitting here, they heard you were coming and going to pass—I have just come from buffalo; I heard you just come out on this prairie—then I think I will go and see you. I want to know what you think. I was talking to my children this past summer—when I found my children were going on war parties I would tell them to stop—be quiet—always tell my people I expect now we will see the chief—I talk to them that way. I expect he will talk to the Blackfeet again. I will stop very soon. I am telling you my mind—stop— wait—when the white man chief talks again you just listen. If the Blackfeet step over their words[31] again we are not afraid of them my children—hold on to your minds my children, look out, danger might come my children—we will just be quiet, they have got arms those we are going to see. If we step over our word to the chief. It is two winters you passed here, every year since my horses have gone to the Blackfeet, last winter one, this spring two. I was going on a war party as your express

30. Stevens, "Pacific Railroad Report," I, 437-438, 441-442. The Blackfeet had broken their promise to Stevens to be friends with the Flatheads, and had stolen horses belonging to Victor's band and had driven them to Fort Benton. Some Kalispells followed and took three horses near the fort in reprisal. Victor refused to accept the horses. Alexander and five companions returned them to Fort Benton in November, 1853. Mullan and Doty describe the incident.

31. Previous verbal agreements of friendship.

passed along here. You say be quiet, I did not go, I will stop and wait—
that is the reason I always stop my children—that is the way I spoke to
my chiefs.

"Now when a chief will talk to the white chief don't be
frightened—we are not going to fight each other, keep on that way; then
I will let go my heart & speak to my children. I am not afraid of my
enemies—you white man, you talk so smoothly, so well, therefore I tell
you I am not ahead of you—I listen to you my father—we all like our
children, take pity on them. Here this spring the Blackfeet put my
daughter on foot—she packed the goods on her back—it made me feel
bad; then I think of what I heard from you my father, and take my heart
back and keep quiet. If I had not listened to your express I would have
gone on war parties over yonder. I thought I would listen good—that is
the reason I always checked those people—my heart said so—I don't
want you to be put in trouble—I don't know your minds, you white
men—I will stop talking. I am not thinking I am talking saucy. I have got
a good deal more to say—I am tired now."

Gov. Stevens said: "I will ask my children if they understand fully what I said yesterday. I asked you if you could agree to go on
one reservation. I ask you now, can you all agree to live on one
reservation? Do you wish to have me speak further on that question. I ask
Victor, are you willing to go on the same reservation with the Pend
'Oreilles and Kootenays? I ask Alexander, are you willing to go on the
same reservation with the Flatheads and Kootenays. I ask Michelle—are
you willing to go on the same reservation with the Flatheads and Pend
'Oreilles? I think a place can be found which will be large enough for you
all. What do you, Victor, Alexander, and Michelle think? You are the
head chiefs. I want you to speak. I understand the Big Canoe to have said
this, "We have always been friends of the whites, we, we have never spilt
his blood, we have always taken the white man by the hand, but we have
suffered for long years from the Blackfeet, our horses have been stolen;
our people killed; we wish it stopt and believe you have come here to
have it stopt. Not that we are afraid of the Blackfeet—no, we will meet
them in battle and drive them before us, but we want to be friends with
all men, Indians and whites, and we are willing to go on the reservations
and receive the aid of the Great Father. We wish, however, to know where
that reservation is, and whether it is a place where we can live." Yes, I

understand the Big Canoe to say, "we are ready all three tribes to go on one reservation, let us know where it is, let us see whether it is large enough." I ask the Big Canoe if I heard him right?"

The Big Canoe said: "I do not understand you right."

Gov. Stevens said: "I now call again upon Victor, Alexander and Michelle and ask them whether they have agreed whether it will be better for all the tribes to go on one reserve if a suitable one can be found? Are you satisfied that it will be better for you and your people to go on one reserve together, or do you [have] objections to it?

"I will ask Victor to speak his mind; whether they have all agreed to go on one reserve, and if so to indicate the place."

Victor said: "I am willing to go on one reservation, but I do not wish to go over yonder[32] (Pend 'Oreille Mission.)"

Alexander said: "It is good for us all to stop in one place."

Michelle said: "I am with Alexander."

Gov. Stevens said: "The Pend 'Oreilles and Kootenays think it will be well to have all the tribes together; perhaps Victor may think so by and by if the place suits. Alexander and Michelle wish to live together—their people on one place; it ought to be a good place—they have a thousand people; the land ought to be good; each man wants his field; the climate ought to be mild—you do not wish your horses to die in the winter; nor do you wish to lose your animals in marshy places; you wish little or no snow in the winter; you want good land for crops; you desire your three thousand animals to increase. Is horse prairie[33] such a place? Is the prairie north of Flathead Lake such a place? There the snow is deep in winter; your horses would die. How is the soil at the Mission? There is Pierre the Iroquois—can he raise crops there?"

Pierre[34] said: "I think so."

Gov. said: "Can all these people raise crops there? There is another place that will suit Victor. It is this valley from Fort Owen[35] to the

32. Meaning the Flathead Valley. The recorder appears to have confused the old mission among the Pend d'Oreilles known as St. Ignatius with the new St. Ignatius Mission in the Flathead Valley.

33. Horse Prairie later was the site of the present town of Plains, Montana. It was at one time known as Wild Horse Plain and the town as Horse Plains, later changed to Plains.

34. Pierre Baptiste was an old Iroquois who lived in the Bitter Root Valley. He had at one time been a trapper and was one of the Iroquois who came into the region with the fur trade.

35. Stevens, "Pacific Railroad Report," I, 257, 293, 437. Seymour Dunbar and Paul C. Phillips, eds., *The Journals and Letters of Major John Owen: Pioneer of the Northwest 1850-1871* (New York, 1927). Fort Owen was a trading post established by Major John Owen, who in 1850 purchased the improve-

upper part. I ask Pierre again, which is the best, this valley or the Mission? He has tried both."

Pierre said: "I do not know."

Governor: "I ask Victor, Alexander and Michelle to think it over: will (they) go to the valley with Victor, or to the mission with Alexander and Michelle: I do not care which. You will have your priest with you whether you go to the mission or Fort Owen; and here I would say those who want the priest can have him. The Great Father means that each one shall do as he pleases in reference to receiving the instructions of the priests; that is the word of the Great Father—each man shall do as he chooses in reference to receiving the instructions of the priests.

"If you live on the reserve as I said yesterday, all your sick will be cared for; we can only give you one physician. All will have a chance to have their wheat ground—we can only give you one grist mill. All will have the same chance to have houses—we can only give you one saw mill. Your farms, your schools, and your shops will be better; you will be better clothed and better provided for every way, because all of you will equally have the care of the agent. The agent will see that we promise to do is done; he is on the ground. Alexander and Michelle live at the mission; Victor lives in this valley. If the agent lives with Victor up the valley can he take care of the business with Alexander and Michelle at the mission? If he lives with Alexander and Michelle at the mission, how can he transact business with Victor up the valley?

"Recollect, you Victor, Alexander & Michelle are chiefs, good chiefs; Victor has not only kept the Blackfeet at bay at Hellgate[36] but has them beyond the mountains. Alexander through the Blackfoot

ments of the St Mary's Mission for his trading venture. The Blackfoot inroads which had directly been responsible for the closing of the mission also caused Owen to vacate the post in 1853. However, he returned to the post when he was assured of the change of Indian affairs by the Stevens party. Owen's journals kept from 1850 to 1871 mention many incidents in the affairs of the Flathead tribe for which he was appointed special Indian agent in 1856.

36. Alexander Ross, *The Fur Hunters of the Far West, A Narrative of Adventures in the Oregon and Rocky Mountains* (London, 1855), II, 12-13. This was a notorious mountain pass and is frequently mentioned in early journals. Alexander Ross in his account of 1823 states, "we reached a defile of the dividing ridge, called Hell's Gates, a distance from Flathead Fort of about 70 miles, general course, S.E. This place is rendered notorious as being the great war-road by which the Piegans and Blackfeet often visit this side of the mountains; by the same pass the Flatheads and other tribes cross over to the Missouri side in quest of buffalo. The spot has, therefore, been the scene of many a bloody contest between these hostile nations."

country carried horses back[37] to Fort Benton; I told the President of it—he knows all about it; and Michelle is a good man ready to fight his enemies and to do what is right. You are chiefs all three, good chiefs, and you will have much to do. If we make a treaty how will the agent know what your people want? He must learn it from Victor, Alexander and Michelle. The chiefs will each year tell the agent what tools, what clothing, what goods they want for their people; what children to go to the school and learn trades, which children shall learn to be blacksmiths, which to be carpenters, which wheelwrights, which farmers. Victor will tell the agent which boy shall learn to be a carpenter, which to be a wheelwright, which to go into the mills, and which girls and boys shall go to school and learn to read and write. It will occupy Victor's whole time; it will Alexander's and Michelle's; they will want to see the agent often—sometimes every day. For the head chiefs of the different tribes we shall build houses and furnish them, and we shall for twenty years pay each head chief a salary of five hundred dollars a year. We do this because you chiefs will be obliged to work for your people and not for yourselves, and we wish to support you properly. Now think over these matters well; agree to come together on one reservation; decide for yourselves whether it shall be the mission or whether it shall be the valley above John Owen's. You shall have either, which you prefer. In the morning we will meet again; then I wish to hear from you; then we can finish the treaty.

"The council is adjourned till tomorrow at 10 o'clock."

The council then adjourned at 6 p.m.

———————

Wednesday, July 11th, 1855.

The Indians assembled at 11 a.m. and at 1/2 past the council opened.

Present the same as yesterday.

Gov. Stevens said: "My children, have you agreed upon the place you will live? I ask the chiefs, I ask Victor."

Victor said, "I am content with the valley."

Gov. "I ask Alexander."

37. Reference to incident in note 30.

Alexander. "The Kootenays and Lower Pend 'Oreilles will come to my place."

Gov. Stevens: "I will speak; I think the best place for you is this valley, from John Owens up the valley. There is more land there for you, the land is better, the climate is milder, you are nearer to camash and bitter root, it is more convenient for buffalo, you will be much better off there, therefore I say, all go there and you will all be glad by and by, if you are not glad now. Will that suit Alexander & Michelle? And here with out rising I will explain one thing. Any improvements will be paid for over and above what is paid for your lands. The labor Pierre has put on his land will be paid for. You can gather your crops. You will not be required to move for a year and a half or two years. The paper has to go to the Great Father; if he thinks it is good, as I think he will, it will be a bargain, but we cannot hear from the Great Father till next year. It will take some time to get tools and seeds and clothing here, to build good mills and shops and start the farms; then you will be called upon to move.

"What does Alexander & Michelle say?"

Alexander: "I don't think so, I think it is too small what you want to give me."

Gov. Stevens: "Alexander, how much smaller is it than where the mission is?"

Alexander: "I think the mission is a larger place."

Gov. Stevens: "Alexander, your agent has seen the place. Lt. Mullan has seen the place; others have seen it (the mission) and they think the place is very much smaller. They have surveyed it, and it is not so good what there is of it, as the place above here. Now you have all said the whites are smarter than you; the white settler would not select that place—it is not good enough. He thinks the valley above Fort Owen is the best place. Now we wish you to have as good a place as the white settler. It would best please the white settler to place you at the mission; we wish you to go where the Great Father thinks it is best for you to go."

Alexander: "There is priest over there, berries, roots, &c."

Gov. Stevens: "The Agent has examined both places; do you know about farms? The agent does. The valley is much the best land."

Alexander: "I cannot go this way—I can't help myself; we are down there at the mission; the Kootenays are there; the Lower Pend 'Oreilles are moving up."

Gov. Stevens: "Are you the chief of the Lower Pend 'Oreilles?"

Alexander: "Yes, I am the chief."

Gov. S. "Who made you the chief of the Lower Pend 'Oreilles?"

Alexander: "I don't know."

Gov. S: "You are not their chief. I shall see the Lower Pend 'Oreilles by and by and talk with them; I am talking to the Upper Pend 'Oreilles."

Alexander: "You inquired if my crops are coming up well—they are doing well."

Gov. S: "How is it with Michelle? Are you willing to go on to the reservation above Fort Owen ?"

Michelle: "I started two years ago from my place to come and see you. These three nations speak one language. I came with Alexander to listen what they would say. That is why I don't talk."

Gov. S: "Michelle wants Victor and Alexander to agree together. He will stand by whatever they do. I told Victor and Alexander yesterday they must agree upon some one spot where they would live together. If they both agree to go to the mission[38] they should go there. If they wished to go above Ft. Owen they should go there. You come here this morning and you do not agree. Victor wants to go above; Alexander to go to the mission; not having agreed I say both go above Ft. Owen; that is the best place. As I said yesterday, if Victor will agree to go to the mission with Alexander, it is enough, he may go. I hope now Alexander will agree to go above here. I know the land; the place is better every way. The council is now adjourned for two hours that you may think it over well."

After the adjournment of the council, Gov. Stevens explained informally to both Alexander and Victor the necessity of placing their tribes together on the same reservation. Alexander said he would agree to go on the reservation in the St. Mary's valley if Gov. S. would say

38. Flathead Valley where the St. Ignatius Mission was located.

he could not go to heaven at his own place. The Gov. replied—"It is not for me to say where you best can go to heaven; you will go to heaven if you do right. It will be best for your children to go to the reservation above Fort Owen." Victor was unwilling to go to the mission. They each would not object to the other coming to his own place.

It being obvious that no progress would be made by continuing the council today, and that an influence was being exerted by the mission which might be adverse to the views of the government, it was determined to despatch [sic] a messenger directing the attendance of Father Hoeken,[39] for the purpose of investigating it; to adjourn the council over to Friday and to recommend the Indians to have a feast and a council tomorrow.

At 3 p.m. the Indians were again assembled, and Gov. Stevens said: "My children; We will have no council tomorrow; we wish you to have a feast together; we wish Alexander and Victor to have a talk together, they speak the same language, they can talk. I have come meaning to do some good for you; I have stated on what terms the government will help you. You must live on one reservation in order to have the aid of the government; that reservation must be there (above Fort Owen). These are the terms of the government; on these we can help you much; you have asked for aid; we have come to give it. You have asked to be protected from the Blackfeet; you *shall* be protected from the Blackfeet, but you must do your part. Go there and the government will protect you; the agent will be there, and many white men whose business it will be to work for you. If the Blackfeet still come we will have soldiers to drive them off. I will tell the Blackfeet this when we meet them. Now these are the terms on which we can aid you, protect you, and provide for your children. One word more—Alexander wants to go to heaven;

39. Adrian Hoecken (1815-1897) was one of the Jesuit missionaries who came to the original St. Mary's Mission among the Flatheads in 1843, two years after its founding. Shortly after he went to the Sacred Heart Mission among the Coeur d'Alenes. In 1844, he founded a mission among the Lower Pend d'Oreilles, which was called St. Ignatius. Dr. George Suckley of the Stevens exploring expedition visited the mission in November, 1853, and was well received by Father Hoecken and others. Father Hoecken was one of the founders of the new St. Ignatius Mission among the Flatheads in 1854 in the Flathead Valley, when the other mission was moved. He signed the Flathead treaty, and also the later Blackfoot treaty. In 1859, he assisted with the founding of St. Peter's Mission among the Blackfeet, and in 1861 went to St. Louis. He is mentioned in Chittenden and Richardson, eds., *Life, . . of Pierre-Jean De Smet;* Dunbar and Phillips, eds., *Journals and Letters of Major Owen;* Stevens, *Stevens;* and Stevens, "Pacific Railroad Report." See note 58 for reference by Stevens in letter.

Hell Gate–Entrance to Cadotte's Pass from the West

Fort Owen–Flathead Village

can he and Victor live together in the next world if they cannot in this? Then in the name of God, live together here; you must live together in the next world, if both go to heaven.

"Now I wish you to have a feast tomorrow; I will provide the means. Think the matter over among yourselves and decide."

The council then adjourned at 4 p.m. till Friday.

Thursday, July 12th.

There was no council today, according to notice. The Indians had a grand feast, the means for which—two beeves, coffee, sugar, &c.—were furnished them; after which the day was spent in discussing the arrangement of the treaty among themselves.

Friday, June [*sic*] 13th.

The Indians assembled at 12 p.m. and after the usual time spent in smoking, the council was opened.

Gov. Stevens said: "My children, you have had your feast; you have counciled together; you have, I am told, nearly agreed. I hope today you will all agree. You were told all go to the valley or all go to the mission. All wished to go to the mission at first except Victor; Victor does not like to leave his land; his children are buried there, but he has children living. His people have children and men will do for their children what they would not do for themselves.

"I ask now, are you ready to go to the mission, and sign the treaty? We must finish the council today; we have other work to do. I am ready now to explain the provisions of the treaty. My children, It is a treaty made between myself acting for the President, and the Flatheads, Kootenays, and Pend 'Oreilles. It provides for a reservation from the Jocko river to the Flathead lake, and from the Flathead river to the mountains. You have the right however to pasture your animals at other places if those places are not occupied by the whites. You have in like manner the right to gather roots and berries, to take fish and kill game. You have also the right to go on the roads of the whites and take your produce to market. The Great Father has the right to make roads through your country if necessary. White people however cannot go there without your consent.

"The treaty provides you with a grist mill and a saw mill; it provides you with a blacksmith's shop, a carpenter's shop, and a wheelwright's and plow-maker's shop; you will have a school, you will have a physician, and especially an agent; and you will have all these things for twenty years. Besides this, we shall the first year expend in clothing, in tools, in building houses, in breaking up and fencing land, thirty six thousand dollars. The next four years we shall expend for the same objects six thousand dollars a year; for the next five years we shall expend for the same objects five thousand dollars; for the next five years four thousand dollars, and for the next five years three thousand dollars. For each head chief we will have a house; and they will be paid five hundred dollars each year for twenty years; The house will be furnished, and ten acres of land will be broken up and fenced for each of them. Those of the Indians who give up improvements outside of the reserve will be paid for their improvements.

"This treaty binds you to be friendly with other tribes, and with the whites. The whites and other tribes will be required to be at peace with you. If a white man takes your property, that property will be restored to you. If you take the property of a white person, that property you will restore to him. The treaty also requires you to refrain from drinking liquor. In making the payments provided for in the treaty, they will be made to each person of the tribe; he will receive his portion into his own hands. If any member of the tribe should be in debt, his indebtedness cannot be drawn by the trader from the several payments; that is a matter to be settled between the parties themselves. This treaty provides not only that no white man shall go on your land, but that no trader shall continue there without your consent. The whole of the land will be yours. (This refers to the paragraph concerning the Hudson Bay Company.[40]) It finally provides that you accept the terms of this treaty as the children of the Great Father, acknowledging your dependence upon him.

"Are you ready to sign the treaty?"

40. See reference in letter, footnote 60.

Alexander said: "I am ignorant; I am an Indian; I am as it were in the dark. I see you here; it is good. I am glad that the Great Father talks about us. I am content with my people. Here you are—are you through with this treaty. Here are the Flatheads. I thought that the Flatheads were willing to go. You named a smaller place and they backed out. When you told us from [about?] the Jocko, they said it was too small. If you had said all on the other side of the mountains perhaps they would have taken it. We are four nations. When the stock increases where will they be? Suppose we put our farms here, where is the room for us."

Gov. Stevens: "You said the other day it was large enough."

Alexander: "I thought all the land on the other side was to be ours."

Gov. S.: "How far do you wish the land to extend? We told Alexander the place was not large enough; he said it was; Victor said it was; believing they could agree we have drawn it up. Do you bear in mind you can pasture your cattle at any place not occupied by whites?"

Alexander: "Sometimes there is a wide open place above filled with animals. I would rather accept the first proposition. When you first talked, you talked good; now you talk sharp; you talk like a Blackfoot."

Gov. Stevens: "I told Alexander I was afraid the place was too small. He said it was sufficiently large even with the Lower Pend 'Oreilles. I said there was a large place; I would rather you would go there. The white settler wants to go above; he does not want your place. You say the white man is smarter than you. I want to give you the place the white man would prefer. You have a feast, you talk with Victor. Victor says that is the best place. I agreed to give you that place; when you say I am sharp, I am like a Blackfoot, I am ashamed of you Alexander; you have changed your mind; you said one thing on yesterday, you say another today. Talk straight and then we will agree."

Alexander: "The Indians said your country is bad below; if one knows how to farm, it will do; if not, it will not do. They said there were few farming spots; they said that the horses would be mixed and lost. I said yes, that is very bad. You (the Gov.) knew it. You have it on paper, and I said it was good. I understand that nobody should put his foot on my ground, then I said I will stay, then nobody shall touch it, before that you never showed me the limits. It is true, it is quite large each side. I think both sides of the Flathead river will just be enough."

Gov. S.: "Are you through?"

Alexander: "I will take from course de femme[41] on both sides of the river to the lake."

Gov. Stevens: "Do you understand that you have the privilege of pasturage for your animals on all lands not occupied by the whites?"

Alexander: "I do not understand perfectly."

Gov. S.: "Do you understand that the treaty secures to you all that land and the benefit ?"

Alexander: "Yes."

Gov. S.: "The treaty gives you the right of pasturage and gathering roots and berries on all lands not occupied by whites."

Alexander: "Yes, I understand, I want the whole land marked out."

(Gov. Stevens again went over the treaty and explained it in all its details.)

Gov. S.: "Now we will sign the treaty."

Alexander: "They did not understand right the provisions—now we understand."

Victor said: "Where is my country: I want to speak."

Gov. S.: "When I call upon you to sign the treaty, you can make your objections."

Victor: "I have not agreed to accept this land (at the mission)."

Gov. S.: "Alexander has agreed and I call upon him."

Victor: "I was talking to you, and I told you no."

Gov. S.: "I now call upon Victor."

Ambrose[42] (Flathead) said: "Yesterday Victor spoke to Alexander. He said, 'I am not headstrong. The whites picked out a place

41. Stevens, "Pacific Railroad Report," I, 517; "Famous Indian Foot Race," *Contributions to the Historical Society of Montana* (Helena, Montana, 1907), VI, 479-480; Arthur L. Stone, *Following Old Trails* (Missoula, Montana, 1913), 32. "Course des Femmes" was so named from the fact that at one time Indian women ran races here. In the 1830s Francis Ermatinger of the Hudson's Bay Company in order to secure the good will of the Flatheads staged foot races for the women and gave attractive prizes.

42. Mullan, *Report on Military Road*, 21. Ambrose was also known as "Amelo" the Indian way of saying his name. He was a friend of the whites and assisted John Mullan with his road in 1860 by

for us, the best place and that is the reason I do not want to go. Two years since they passed us—now the white man has his foot on our ground—the white man will stay with you—this is what I heard two years ago.' Yesterday when we had the feast then Alexander spoke; he said now I will go over to your side. I will let them take my place and come to your place. Then Victor did not speak and the council broke up."

Gov. S.: "Alexander, did you agree yesterday to give up your country and join Victor?"

Alexander: "Yes yesterday I did give up. I listened and he did not give me an answer; then I said I will not give up my land."

Gov. S.: "I speak now to the Pend 'Oreilles and the Kootenays. Do you agree to this treaty? The treaty placing the Kootenays and Pend 'Oreilles on this reservation? I ask Victor if he declines to treat."

Victor: "Talk, I have nothing to say now."

Gov. S.: "Does Victor want to treat? Why did he not say to Alexander yesterday, come to my place? or is not Victor a chief? Is he as one of his people has called him, an old woman? dumb as a dog? If Victor is a chief let him speak now."

Victor: "I thought my people perhaps you would listen—I said, I think this is my country and all over here is my country. Some of my people want to be above here. I sit quiet and before me you give my land away. If I thought so I would tell the whites to take the land there (the mission); it is my country. Long time ago you spoke to me here; then I thought I was very well pleased. I thought no one would touch it because you talked about it and I liked this place myself. I am listening and my people say take my country."

Gov. S.: "Alexander said yesterday that he would come up here. Why did you not answer and say come?"

Victor: "Yesterday I did talk."

Gov. S.: "Alexander says yesterday he offered to give up his land and come to you—Alexander says you made no answer. Why did you not say, yes, come to my place."

Victor: "I did not understand it so."

supplying him with more than one hundred horses and about twenty men to bring needed supplies from Fort Benton to the Bitter Root Valley.

Gov. S.: "Ambrose says he understood Alexander to say so. Alexander says he said so; you did not speak and say come to my place; but you were dumb—did not say a word."

Victor: "I do not insist upon staying here, but because you picked out my place[43] I want to stay here."

Gov. S.: "Why did you not tell Alexander to come to my place; does Victor mean to say that he will neither let Alexander come to his place nor go to Alexander's."

Ambrose: "The Great Father will know what we are talking about. We get a little stick and shove at it, perhaps we will hit it after a while. Here we are yet. If the paper is sent to the Great Father he will say here is a fool and here is a smart man; if the Great Father sees the fool's paper he will not be pleased (alluding to the notes taken). I say to the white chief, don't get angry, may be it will come all right. May be all the people have a great many minds, may be they will come all right. See my chiefs are now holding down their heads, thinking."

Tilcoostay (Flathead) said: "It is not our minds that we see each other here; your fore fathers did not expect to make a treaty; God is working it this way. His children are very poor; they are lost; only from their tongues, they work it different ways. We are all brothers, but we speak different tongues, that is all, and the color of our skins; we are all brothers, that is why you are travelling here. They are poor, these people; they don't know how to talk; a wolf can't talk; take pity on your children—I am done talking."

Red Wolf[44] said: "I talked the other day and the Indians said I talked as though I was telling a story. I am proud, let them laugh at me, I am going to speak. Yesterday when we talked about this we studied all round—Victor is head chief and I am far below him. When we gathered up the first time I thought that he was making up his mind to stop at Flathead lake, but now he makes up his mind to stop here. Alexander spoke yesterday saying now I let it go—now I will come to the Bitter Root valley—I understood him so yesterday. I know Victor's heart, he does not speak quick—Alexander went off. I thought that Victor would agree and that we would all go there. I thought Victor would agree and would speak soon. Victor did not speak—I think this is the cause Victor did not talk,

43. Bitter Root Valley, home of the Flatheads.
44. See reference, footnote 25.

he was not ready to talk. Big Canoe talked then. He spoke as though a hand had been placed on Victor's mouth, that is the reason I think why Victor did not speak. I went home and told my lodge that I thought our people would come together. Now when the people separated Alexander spoke. I know that if Alexander should come to the valley his people would not follow him. I think when Victor should talk if he did talk in favor of the other side all his children called Flatheads, it would all be right. I think if Victor goes there, though his people will not like to follow him, he cannot take it back and his people will have to go. I think that Victor is the head chief; we are in the same place that we were at first. I have no share in this country—my father's land is below—my mother's country is here. The Kootenays are my relations. This is my opinion— They dislike to leave their country."

Beartrack[45] said: "We are trying to make a treaty. I will speak to you as though you were the Great Father. We met each other— you are my chief—we talked—when we talked we did not talk above or below, only one thing we talked about, we talked about what we wished to get. I want an agent—I want a doctor—I want a teacher—I want a farmer, a blacksmith, this is what we were talking about. Our chief (Lt. Mullan) says look at this just as though it were before eyes. I looked at it and I was content and glad. He was on his horse, I told him to get down, I was glad, I wanted help, that is what I was talking about, then I spoke, 'I tell you, my chief, you know me I am suffering, what for? My enemies.' He said, 'Ah, I will help you,' he said 'my people are coming, you will see them.' I said, I am glad, I will look for them. Now we see each other—you are my chief and father. You spoke; they have two minds, I am lost, I am very sorry. I might as well lie down, I am ashamed my father. I have considered, I am poor, I made up my mind, I will talk, I will show my mind. I speak as though to the Great Father, I will talk about the land. I think there is only one thing I am sorry for, I have a very poor country. I do not know what to do if my father tells me to go away. There are my old people I am sleeping with them; when they rise I rise. I think there is only one thing that we cover ourselves with. I studied. I am poor. I

45. William T. Hamilton, "A Trading Expedition Among the Indians in 1858 from Fort Walla Walla to the Blackfoot Country and Return," *Contributions to the Historical Society of Montana,* (Helena, Montana, 1900), III, 33-123. Bear Track signed the treaty here being made and also that with the Blackfeet later. He was a sub-chief of the Flatheads. In 1858, he accompanied William T. Hamilton on a trading expedition to the Blackfoot country.

looked at my children. What will I do with my children? What will they be? It appears to me there is not room enough at the mission. You might as well tell me to go far to a big place. My country is about as large as my finger nail. I look at my nail; if I break it, it will not be good—something big it is good for me to break; this [is] my mind and the reason my heart is heavy. If you wish you are my father, tell me, break off your piece of land. I look over my country and study about it. May be I would break it off—I say yes, good. You my father, I think it is not bad making this treaty; it would [be] good to make this treaty; this my mind; this is what I am telling you."

Gov. Stevens: "Ambrose, I am glad you think it is good to make a treaty; the treaty that we make will make you better off. The land reservation is much more than the same number of whites would want. We wish you to live together so that the agent can attend to you. When I met other tribes, many did not want to leave their lands, but they have made up their minds and all gone. I will tell you what a great chief said on the other side—he said, I do not want schools, farms, or mills, but my people want farms, schools and mills and they want to make a treaty; I therefore will make a treaty and he did make a treaty, and his people approved and signed with him. He was a Yakima chief—Kameiakan.[46] I hope Victor will do as Kameiakan did—I hope Victor's people will do as Kameiakan's people. Owhi signed the treaty also—you know him. Trust your father and trust your chiefs.

"My children, I find that things are nearer to an agreement than when we began talking this morning. Ambrose says the people are not quite prepared, they will be by and by; and Ambrose says be patient and listen. I am patient and have been patient and have listened to them. Others of you have said they were hiding their thought (minds) and did not speak; hence I reproved you and said speak out—let me have your hearts. It seems that many of the Flatheads are ready to go to the mission; if their chief says so, they will go. Victor says I am ready to go, but my

46. A. J. Splawn, *Ka-mi-akin, The Last Hero of the Yakimas* (Portland, Oregon, 1917); Benjamin F. Manring, *The Conquest of the Coeur d' Alenes, Spokanes and Palouses* (Spokane, Washington, 1912). Both Kamiakan and Owhi signed the treaty with the Yakima tribe, June 9, 1855. Kamiakan was made head chief of his nation. Following the treaty, Indian disturbance as the result of misunderstandings about the treaty took place (1856-1858) which caused Kamiakan to take refuge in British Columbia, Owhi's son Quelchin to be hung, and Owhi to die of a wound caused by gunfire when he tried to escape detention.

people will not, but the people say they are ready to go. We want all parties to speak straight, to let us have their hearts, then we can agree. If Victor's people will go, we want Victor as chief to say I will go."

Victor here arose and left the council. After a pause of some minutes Gov. Stevens said: "I will ask Ambrose where is Victor?"

Ambrose: "He is gone home."

Gov. Stevens: "Ambrose speaking of Victor said he wanted time. Victor is now thinking and studying over this matter. We don't wish to hurry or drive you in this business. Think over this matter tonight and meet here tomorrow. I ask Ambrose to think over the matter; to speak to Victor and tell him what I say. Ambrose loves his chief—let him take my words to him."

The council is adjourned to meet tomorrow morning somewhat earlier than usual.

The council then adjourned at 5 p.m.

———————

Saturday, June [*sic*] 14th.

Word was sent by Victor about 3 o'clock p.m. to the Governor that he had not yet made up his mind; and that as it was too late to open the council, it was postponed till Monday morning.

———————

Monday, June [*sic*] 16th.

The council was opened at 11 a.m., present as before.

Gov. Stevens said: "My children, at the council Friday we did not succeed in agreeing. Victor as chief of his people required more time to consider; he did [not] wish to act hastily; his people wanted time to think. The next day I saw Alexander but I did not see Victor. Victor was still studying and thinking what he should do. Alexander then had word sent to Victor "you shall be my chief if you will come to my place." Victor said, "I do not wish to speak today. I will come tomorrow and then speak."

Victor said: "I am going to talk; I was not content—you gave me a very small place; then I thought, here they are giving away my land. That is my country over there at the mission; this also—I think so; plenty of you say Victor is the chief; you white people say so too—Victor is the chief of the Flatheads. Two years ago you passed here, then you gave me a flag[47]; it was very small, we thought it very big. It came from you. I thought then we had make [made] a kind of treaty. The place you pointed to me above is too small: from Lou-Lou[48] fork above should belong to me. My stock will have room, and if the Blackfeet will let my horses alone they will increase. I believe that you wish to help me and that my (children) people will do well there. If you want we will [send] this word to the Great Father our chief—come and look at our country: perhaps you will choose that place if you look at it. When you look at Alexander's place and say the land is good, and say, come Victor—then I would go. If you think this above is good land, then Victor will say come here Alexander; then our children will be well content. That is the way we will make the treaty, my father."

Gov. Stevens "Victor has spoken; does Alexander and Michelle speak in the same way?

"I will ask Alexander if he agrees?"

Alexander: "If I do say yes, I am content, may be we can't all come together. Here is Michelle, I know his mind, he told me—'if you go this way I won't go.' Here are the Lower Pend 'Oreilles; may be they are the same way. They have no horses; they have only canoes. I am very heavy as though they tied me there."

Gov. S.: "Victor says I want the Great Father to have both places examined. If the Great Father says that[49] is the best place, I, Victor, will go there. If the Great Father says this is the best place then Michelle and Alexander will come to me. Victor wants both places examined, so the Great Father will know which is the best—there let all the Indians go.

"I will say to Alexander, both places shall be carefully examined. Alexander shall show every thing about his place—Victor about his. The Lower Pend 'Oreilles will want to go to the best place, and we promise them in the treaty to give them animals to go to the best place. Victor thinks all will be satisfied with what proves after examination to be the best place. I ask Alexander whether he is content with this proposition of Victor's."

47. The American Flag.
48. In the Bitter Root Valley. "Lolo" is the accepted spelling today.
49. "That" refers to the Flathead Valley; "this" to the Bitter Root.

Alexander: "I think not so—I have not seen the chief of the Lower Pend 'Oreilles but I will speak to him."

Gov. S.: "I say to Alexander, he is here chief of the Upper Pend 'Oreilles, I shall see Victor the chief of the Lower Pend d'Oreilles and talk to him myself. The chief of the Lower Pend d'Oreilles will be bound only by what he agrees to. We cannot act for him; he is not here. Victor of the Flatheads, Alexander and Michelle are here; it is with them I am treating. Here are two places; Victor wants them both examined. Let the Great Father say which is the best place, I will go there. We want you to agree some way or other; we wish you to agree among yourselves. I have asked Alexander already. I wish to think more. I will ask Michelle."

Alexander said: "The way I think of it I don't think we will come together."

Gov. S.: "Will Michelle agree to Victor's proposal, that the Indians shall go to the best place after the Great Father has examined both and says which is the best place."

Michelle said: "I am just following Alexander's mind. If he goes this way I will not go. I have come a long way to see you; when you leave I go back."

Gov. S.: "Victor has said that he would go to the best place that which was found to be the best after examination. Alexander and Michelle both say that they are willing to go to the mission—they will not go any where's else. Victor is willing to go there if it should be the best place. Is Victor willing to say that he is willing to go to the mission in order to agree with Alexander and Michelle." Victor adhered to his proposition.

Gov. S. continued after a short pause: "My children, Victor has made his proposition, Alexander and Michelle have made theirs. We will make a treaty for them. Both tracts shall be surveyed; if the mission is the best land Victor shall live there. If this valley is the best land Victor shall stay here. Alexander and Michelle may stay at the mission. I cannot say that the President will think it good. The President will think it very strange Alexander and Michelle are not willing to leave it to him. I will however sign the treaty with them. If the President thinks it good then we shall carry it out—if he thinks it not good then we shall not carry it out. I am now ready to sign.

"Ask Victor if he understands; I will explain it anew. Both reserves shall be surveyed and the surveys sent to the President. If the President thinks over there (the mission) is the best place, Victor will go there; if up the valley the best—Victor will stay. Alexander and Michelle will remain at the mission. Here is the treaty drawn up. I have written out what I have just explained. I ask Victor to come up and sign the treaty.[50] (He came up and signed.)

"Now I ask Alexander and Michelle." (They also then signed.)

Moses (Flathead) on being asked to sign the treaty stepped forward and said: "My brother is buried there. I did not think you would take the only piece of ground I had. Here are three fellows (the chiefs), they say get on your horse and go; they never say talk. If you would give us a big place I would not talk foolish. If I go in your country and say give me this, will you give it to me. May be you know it—here is all of these people—they have only one piece of ground. Now their mouths are all shut—sewed up. Last year when you were talking about the Blackfeet you were joking."

Gov. Stevens: "How can Moses say that I am not going to the Blackfeet country? I have gone all the way to the Great Father to arrange about the Blackfeet council. What more can I do? A man is coming from the Great Father to meet me. Does he not know that Mr. Burr[51] and another man went to Fort Benton the other day."

Moses: "You have pulled all my wings off and let me down there."

Gov. Stevens: "All that we have done is for your benefit. I have said the Flatheads were brave and honest and should be protected—be patient—every thing will come right."

Moses: "I do not know how it will be straight—a few days ago the Blackfeet stole horses at Salmon River. Here is Ben—last winter he went to the fort—he had some people there."

Gov. S.: "Ask him if he sees the Nez Perce chief—The Eagle from the Light[52]; he is going to the Blackfeet council with me."

50. This treaty is given in full in Kappler, *Indian Treaties*, 722-725.

51. Fred H. Burr, a member of the exploring party, who in 1856 went into the cattle business in western Montana.

52. "Eagle from the Light" signed the treaty June 11, 1855, with his Indian name of Tippleanacbupooh. He later was one of the dissatisfied chiefs because of incidents growing out of treaty arrangements.

Bitter Root River near Fort Owen

Victor's Camp–Hell Gate Ronde

Moses: "Yes, I see him; they will get his hair."

Gov. S.: "They will have to get my scalp too. I am not afraid."

Moses: "The Blackfeet are not like these people; they are all drunk."

Gov. S.: "The Blackfeet will sign a treaty to keep the peace; we do not bring soldiers here, we are all friends; we do not wear knives here."

Moses: "You left a man here (Lt. Mullan); he said they will never talk about this land—they will help you against the Blackfeet. That is the reason we all came together."

Gov. S.: "Ask him if Victor is not his head chief?"

Moses: "Yes, but I never listen to him. Will you give me land if I go to your country?"

Gov. S.: "Yes, as much as you choose to buy."

Moses: "Don't give your goods to these people; give them to the Blackfeet."

Gov. S.: "We will give you mills, &c. That is the kind of house we will give you."

Moses: "Now I understand, (he here gave his adherence to the treaty, though still refusing[53] to sign.) I have nothing to say about selling the land."

The principal men then came forward and signed; after which

Gov. Stevens said: "Here are three papers which you have signed, copies of the same treaty; one goes to the President; one I place in the hands of the head chief; and one I keep myself. Every thing that has been said here goes to the President.

"I have now a few presents for you; they are simply as a gift; no part of the payments; the payments cannot be made till we hear from the President next year. As soon as Mr. Adams arrives from Fort Owen the goods will be distributed."

A few minutes after Mr. Adams having arrived, the goods were distributed. The chiefs were then informed that all business was

---

53. His signature appears on the official treaty.

through with regard to this council; but that tomorrow they would be assembled with regard to the Blackfeet council.[54]

The council then adjourned sine die, at 5 p.m.

Approved.

    Isaac I. Stevens
Gov. & Supt. W.T. &
    Commissioner.

      I hereby certify the above to be a true record of the official proceedings at the council held in the Bitter Root Valley with the Flathead, Kootenay & Upper Pend 'Oreille tribes of Indians, and concluded this 16th day of July 1855.

                James Doty
                Secretary Treaties.

****

Cover letter for Council Proceedings

                Council Ground at Hell Gate,
                Bitter Root Valley, W.T.
                July 16th, 1855.

Hon. Geo. W. Manypenny[55]
Commissioner of Indian Affairs,
Washington, D. C.

Sir:

      I have this day concluded a Treaty with the Flathead, Kootenay and Upper Pend Oreilles Tribes of Indians, and herewith enclose a copy of the Treaty and the record of the official proceedings.

      These three tribes number some fourteen hundred souls; Flatheads, 450, Kootenays 350 and Upper Pend Oreilles 600. They own about 3500 horses and one thousand cattle.

54. Partoll, ed., "The Blackfoot Indian Council," gives the proceedings of this assembly.
55. He later wrote a book on Indian affairs: *Our Indian Wards* (Cincinnati, 1880) .

Their country embraces an area of about 23,000 square miles. The Reservation on the Flathead River an area of about 2000 square miles.

These tribes are by the Treaty consolidated into one Nation, with Victor the Chief of the Flatheads, as Head Chief of the nation. Provision is made in the Treaty for uniting with them other friendly Tribes. It is expected that the Coeur d'Alene and Lower Pend Oreilles, each numbering about 350 souls, will agree to be thus disposed of.

Much difficulty was experienced in bringing the Tribes on to one Reservation in consequence of the dislike of the Flatheads to mission establishments.[56] Victor finally made a proposition in council today, which I accepted, providing for the survey of the Bitter Root Valley above the Loo-lo Fork, and guaranteeing to the Flatheads a separate Reservation in that valley, should it prove to be better adapted to the wants of his people than the Reservation on the Flathead River. To this latter Reservation he and his people have agreed to go, should it prove to be more eligible than that in the Bitter Root Valley.

Accordingly Article Eleventh was inserted in the Treaty, making provision for this survey, and leaving the question of their Reservation to be settled by the President.

The Chiefs of the Upper Pend Oreilles and Kootenays were unwilling to leave the selection of their Reservation to the President, but declined treating unless they were placed on the Flathead River Reservation.

The Reservation provided for in the Treaty will accordingly be carefully examined and the information thus gained will be laid before the Department at the earliest practicable period. Should the Flathead River Reservation prove best, there will be no difficulty in the premises. Should the Bitter Root Reservation prove most eligible, it will be for the President and Senate to determine whether the Treaty shall be ratified[57] without an amendment requiring all the Tribes to go upon the Reservation, which on examination has been found most eligible.

56. This appears to be a mistaken idea since it was the Flathead Valley that Victor wished to avoid as a reservation. He preferred his home in the Bitter Root Valley.

57. "Report of Secretary of Interior, 1870," *House Executive Documents,* 41 Cong., 3 Sess., no. 1, 656-660. [ser. 1449]; *Fourth Annual Report of the Board of Indian Commissioners . . . 1872* (Washington, 1872), 7-8, 171-174, 186; Oliver W. Holmes, ed., "James A. Garfield's Diary of a Trip to Montana in 1872," *Frontier and Midland* (Winter, 1934-35), XV, 159-168; Stone, *Old Trails,* 83-90. Governmental

I prepared the Indians for this latter alternative in my remarks today, which will be found in the official proceedings, by saying to them, the Treaty might not be ratified in consequence of the refusal of the Kootenay and Upper Pend Oreilles Chiefs to agree to the selection of their Reservation by the President, and I carefully explained the whole matter to Father Hoecken,[58] the Jesuit Missionary, whose presence I had required at the Treaty Ground, and whose influence over these Indians is almost unbounded. The mission is on the Flathead River Reservation on the Si-ni-el-le-em[59] River, to which place it has been removed from below the Pend Oreille Lake within the last twelve months. Father Hoecken has labored faithfully among the Indian Tribes for the last ten years, and has gained his influence by energy, devotion and the natural ascendency of a patient and indomitable will. He has promised to interpose lo [no] obstacle whatever to the views of the government, and I have confidence in his singleness of purpose.

Article 9th [10] of the Treaty guarantees the Indians the undisturbed possession of their Reservation as against the claims of the Hudson Bay Company growing out of their Trading post[60] on the Pruin[61]

---

relations with the Flathead nation may be followed in the *Annual Reports of the Commissioner of Indian Affairs* and in Dunbar and Phillips, eds., *Journals and Letters of Major Owen.* Maps illustrating treaty reservations are to be found in Charles C. Royce, "Indian Land Cessions in the United States," *Eighteenth Annual Report of the Bureau of American Ethnology . . . 1896-'97* (Washington, 1899), Part II, maps 39 and 40. The treaty was ratified, March 8, 1859, and proclaimed, April 18, 1859. Action on article eleven was not taken until 1872 when the Honorable James A. Garfield, special commissioner, took up the matter in August, 1872. Civilization had in the meanwhile moved into the valley of the Bitter Root and settlement had begun without authorization from Washington, apparently not in keeping with the spirit of the treaty. A part of the tribe consented to the terms of removal, but Chief Charlot, Victor's son, would not be reconciled to the terms. He remained in the valley he claimed as his home until October, 1891, when his own poverty and that of his people induced him to move to the reservation in the Flathead Valley.

58. See footnote 39 for biographical sketch.

59. This name means "surrounded" or the "place that is surrounded," and is thought to take its name from a sheltered place enclosed by mountains. Tradition relates that a band of Blackfeet Indians were surrounded by the Flathead Indians there, and that deer and elk were hunted by surrounding them there. Another version is that the name was given the place because it means meeting place or rendezvous. The stream running from this canyon took this name, but was later called Mission Creek because St. Ignatius Mission was located on it.

60. Fort Connah, the Flathead Post of the Hudson's Bay Company, was the last post of the company to do business in the United States. It was closed in 1871 by Chief Trader Angus McDonald at the direction of the company. The Flathead treaty (Article 10) reads: "The United States further agree to guaranty the exclusive use of the reservation provided for in this treaty, as against any claims which may be urged by the Hudson Bay Company under the provisions of the treaty between the United States

River within the limits of the Reservation. It consists simply of three old and small log houses. Not over two acres of land has ever been cultivated. An estimate will be submitted of its value in my annual report. Notice will be given to cease trading with the Indians at that Post, and if persisted in the buildings will be torn down and the Traders sent out of the Indian Country.

The remaining articles of the Treaty require no further explanation, as similar provisions were embodied in the Treaty already ratified, and those which have been subsequently made.

> I am, Sir,
> Very respectfully
> Your Most Obedient Servant
> Isaac I. Stevens
> Governor & Supt. Indn. Affairs
> Washington Territory.[62]

and Great Britain of the fifteenth of June, eighteen hundred and forty-six, in consequence of the occupation of a trading-post on the Pruin River by the servants of that company."

61. Kappler, *Indian Treaties*, 725, as quoted in footnote 60, records this stream as "Pru-in" which may be a misprint. This stream is called "Post" Creek today.

62. Stevens' next treaty was with the Blackfeet in October, 1855, which was to be of great significance in the history of the Pacific Northwest. "In many ways the Blackfoot Indian council corresponded to the international peace tribunals of the white men. Warriors who had previously met only on the field of battle, or had taken part in expeditions for plundering each other, forgot their past differences to listen to the words of the "Great Soldier Chief," as Stevens was titled by the Indians. Wise tribal councillors chose to arbitrate with diplomacy not force. Statesmanship was preferable to the chaos of battle." Partoll, ed., "The Blackfoot Indian Council," Introduction.

66

Pend d'Oreilles Mission in the Rocky Mountains in 1862

Gustavus Sohon's Portraits of Flathead and Pend d'Oreille Indians, 1854

by John C. Ewers

GUSTAVUS SOHON'S PORTRAITS OF FLATHEAD INDIAN LEADERS

The series of nine pencil portraits of Flathead leaders, drawn by Gustavus Sohon in the Bitterroot Valley in the spring of 1854, includes the likenesses of the majority of the responsible leaders of that remarkable little tribe in the middle of the nineteenth century. Most of these men were born before their tribe met white men. All were well known to the Catholic missionaries who founded St. Mary's Mission, and many of them were mentioned prominently in the writings of Father De Smet and his colleagues. They comprised the majority of the Flathead leaders who negotiated the tribe's first and only treaty with the United States a year after Sohon drew these portraits. Many of them also signed the important Blackfoot Treaty of 1855.

In the following biographical sketches of the subjects of Mr. Sohon's portraits, the artist's own brief but informative characterizations, written in his own hand on the same sheets as the portraits, are printed in smaller type beneath the name of the subject.

From John C. Ewers, *Gustavus Sohon's Portraits of Flathead and Pend d'Oreille Indians, 1854.* Smithsonian Miscellaneous Collections, volume 110, number 7 (1948) p. 27-43, 47-54, 57-62, and 64-66.

Victor —

VICTOR, THE PRINCIPAL FLATHEAD CHIEF

Victor—
Head Chief of the Flatheads—

Victor has been confused by some writers with a contemporary of the same Christian name who was head chief of the Lower Pend d'Oreille. Father Palladino said that the Indians called the Flathead Victor "Mitt to" and the Pend d'Oreille one "Pitol" to distinguish them. (Palladino, 1894, p. 63.) Pierre Pichette translated Victor's Indian name "Easy to Get a Herd of Horses." (See also Teit, 1930, p. 377.)

Victor said that he had been quite a good-sized boy when Lewis and Clark passed through the Flathead country in 1805 on their way to the Pacific. His father, Three Eagles, is said to have been a chief of the Flathead camp met by Lewis and Clark. (Owen, 1927, vol. 2, p. 42; Wheeler, 1904, vol. 2, p. 65.)

Victor's early years were molded by traditional Flathead religious beliefs. Pierre Pichette said that in his youth Victor obtained rabbit power by protecting a rabbit which was chased by a hawk. Some years later while stealing horses from the Crow, Victor was thrown from a stolen horse in the midst of the enemy encampment. He ran and hid in some brush near the camp. Although the Crow searched for him all through the next day they could not find him. The following evening Victor escaped. His rabbit power is credited with having saved him.

Victor was a minor leader of the Flathead when Father De Smet and his colleagues founded St. Mary's Mission. He was among the first Indians to accept Christianity and became the leader of the men's society organized by the priests. Agnes, his wife, led the women's society. Father De Smet credited Victor's leadership in the Catholic society as an important factor in his choice by the tribe as head chief, after the death of the octogenarian, Big Face, in late 1841 or early 1842. De Smet said Victor obtained tribal leadership "for no other reason" than "for the noble qualities, both of heart and head, which they all thought he possessed."

In the summer of 1846 Victor led the Flathead buffalo hunt to the plains, during which his people, augmented by 30 lodges of Nez Perce and a dozen friendly Blackfoot, scored a signal victory in a battle with the Crow. (Chittenden and Richardson, 1905, vol. 2, pp. 576-577.)

Later that fall Victor took a prominent part in Father De Smet's negotiation of a peace between the Flathead and Blackfoot at the Piegan camp. De Smet was impressed by Victor's oratory at the meeting of the head men of the tribes in the priest's lodge:

> Victor, head chief of the Flatheads, by the simplicity and smoothness of his conversation gains the good will of his hearers entirely. He begins by telling some of his warlike adventures; but as is easy to see, much less with the intention of exalting himself than to show forth the protection that the true God always grants to those who devote themselves to his service. [Ibid., p. 592.]

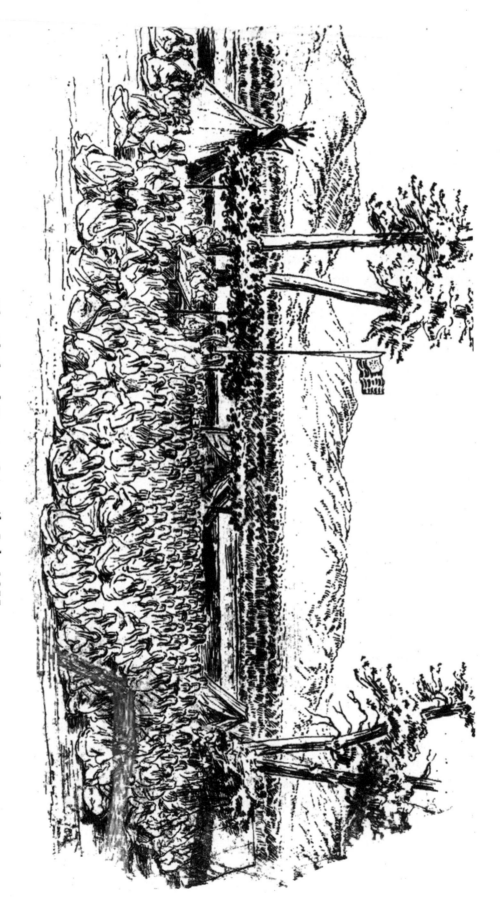

The Flathead Treaty Council, July 1855
—by Gustavus Sohon

Gustavus Sohon

1825-1903

These portraits of Flathead and Pend d'Oreille leaders were drawn in 1854 by Gustavus Sohon while he served in Lt. John Mullan's exploration party in Western Montana.

Born in Germany in 1825, Sohon emigrated to the United States in 1842 and enlisted in the United States Army in 1852. Sohon took part as an enlisted man in Isaac I. Stevens' railroad survey in Western Montana in 1853 and 1854. Mullan and a party of 15 men, including Sohon, were left in the Bitterroot Valley during the winter of 1853-1854 to make weather observations and conduct additional geographic explorations. Sohon was a gifted linguist and rapidly learned to speak Salish. In the process he compiled a Flathead-English vocabulary of some 1,500 useful words. During this stay in Western Montana he produced most of the pencil drawings which are reproduced here.

Sohon was attached to Stevens' party during the treaty negotiation trip of 1855 and served with Ben Kiser, a mixedblood Shawnee-white who lived with the Salish, as an official interpreter at the Hell Gate Treaty negotiations with the Salish and Kootenai. Father Adrian Hoecken, S.J., later disparaged the quality of the interpreting work at the treaty council. Sohon did become friends with a number of Salish leaders. A Salish delegation unsuccessfully requested in 1866 that Sohon be appointed Indian agent for the tribes. In 1884, while on a visit to Washington, DC, Charlo, Victor's son and successor, paid a personal call on Sohon at his home.

After the treaty negotiations, Sohon served at different northwest army posts until his discharge in 1857. From 1858 to 1862 Sohon worked in various capacities with Mullan, building the Mullan Road from Fort Benton to Walla Walla.

Sohon's later years were spent doing photographic work in California and operating a shoe business in Washington, DC. He died in 1903 leaving a unique collection of artistic documents about Indian life and leaders in the Pacific Northwest of the 1850s.

For further biographical information see John C. Ewers, *Gustavus Sohon's Portraits of Flathead and Pend d'Oreille Indians, 1854,* Smithsonian Miscellaneous Collections, volume 110, number 7 (1948) and John C. Ewers, *Artists of the Old West* (Doubleday & Company, Garden City, NY, 1973) p. 172-181.—**Bigart and Woodcock.**

Among the many causes of the disaffection of the Flathead that led to the closure of St. Mary's Mission in 1850, Father Accolti mentioned the loss of influence of the chiefs following the abolishment of the punishment of the whip. (Garraghan, 1938, vol. 2, p. 382.) In the face of rising dissatisfaction with his leadership, Victor clung to his decision not to use the whip. Victor's close identification with the missionaries and his known piety also served to make him a target for abuse by the dissatisfied element. He deplored his people's change of heart, but seemed powerless to prevent it. Father Accolti wrote in the fall of 1852 that Victor had become only a nominal chief, especially since he had permitted a rival to strike him in the face without retaliating. (Ibid., p. 387.)

Governor Stevens visited Victor at Fort Owen in early October, 1853. He briefly recorded his impressions of the Flathead chief: "He appears to be simple-minded, but rather wanting in energy, which might, however, be developed in an emergency." (Report of Explorations, etc., 1860, vol. 12, pt. I, p. 123.) Apparently that emergency was at hand the next time these two met, at the Flathead Treaty Council in the summer of 1855. When he visited Stevens 2 days before the formal Council opened, Victor complained of the failure of the Blackfoot to keep the peace promised by their chiefs 2 years earlier. He informed Stevens that 12 Flathead hunters had been killed by the Blackfoot and many horses stolen since the Blackfoot chiefs agreed to a peace. He mentioned that the Blackfoot had stolen horses seven times that spring. "Now I listen and hear what you wish me to do. Were it not for you I would have had my revenge ere this." (Partoll, 1938, p. 286.)

It must have been a shock to Victor to find, after the Council opened, that Governor Stevens talked of land cessions and the placement of the Indians on a reservation, rather than of a solution to the pressing problem of Blackfoot depredations. Nevertheless, he retained his faith in Stevens' good intentions. "I believe you wish to assist me to help my children here so that they may have plenty to eat, and so that they may save their souls." Although Victor claimed as his land the Flathead River country to the north occupied by the Upper Pend d'Oreille, as well as the Bitterroot Valley, he insisted that it was not a large tract. "There is a very little land here: I cannot offer you a large piece." (Ibid., p. 289.)

Victor was willing for all the tribes to go on one reservation but would not consider moving to the Flathead Valley. Alexander, the Upper Pend d'Oreille chief, preferred the northern location. In an effort to break the deadlock, Stevens expressed an opinion that the Bitterroot Valley was the better site because its climate was milder, it was nearer to camas and bitterroot, and more convenient for buffalo. But he could not convince Alexander. Hoping that time for private discussion might provide a solution to the problem, Governor Stevens declared the next day a holiday on which he feasted the Indians.

When the Council reconvened, Stevens believed majority sentiment favored the northern location. Therefore, he again described the treaty provisions and proposed a reservation within an area bounded by the Jocko River, Flathead Lake, Flathead River, and the mountains. He called on Victor to sign the treaty. Victor refused.

Then the Flathead chief, Ambrose, revealed that on the preceding day Alexander had approached Victor with an offer to move to the Bitterroot Valley, but Victor had refused to answer the Pend d'Oreille chief. After hearing this, Stevens lost patience with Victor and spoke sharply: "Does Victor want to treat? Why did he not say to Alexander yesterday, come to my place? or is not Victor a chief? Is he as one of his people has called him, an old woman? dumb as a dog? If Victor is a chief let him speak now."

Probably angry and somewhat confused, Victor replied that he had not understood Alexander's offer, that he recalled Governor Stevens had himself chosen the Bitterroot Valley as the better location. Then the lesser Flathead chiefs sought to explain Victor's silence of the previous day, stressing the variety of opinion among the Flathead, Victor's habitual thoughtfulness and slowness of speech. Probably Red Wolf stated the matter precisely when he said, "I know that if Alexander should come to the valley, his people would not follow him." Doubtless Victor had no more faith in the practicality of Alexander's offer. While the others continued to talk, Victor quietly walked out of the Council.

Governor Stevens decided to give Victor more time to consider. Next day, Saturday, Victor sent word that he had not made up his mind. The Council was postponed until Monday. (Ibid., pp. 301-308.)

Victor faced probably the most difficult problem of his life. He had agreed to the one reservation proposal. He knew, on the one hand, that Alexander's people were loath to leave the Mission and might not follow their chief if he agreed to move to the Bitterroot Valley. On the other hand, Victor knew that his own people were divided in their opinion. Moise, the Flathead second chief, was opposed to any land cession whatever. Bear Track, the powerful medicine man, refused to leave the Bitterroot Valley. Many of his people were still hostile to Missions and might refuse to follow him if he agreed to move to a reservation near St. Ignatius. His own position as chief was not strong. Should he make an unpopular decision, that position might be lost. Not only his own future but that of his tribe was at stake. Victor refused to be stampeded or shamed into a decision.

When the Council reopened on July 16, Victor offered a masterful compromise. He proposed that Governor Stevens send "this word to the Great Father our Chief—come and look at our country; perhaps you will choose that place if you look at it. When you look at Alexander's place and say this land is good, and say, come Victor—then I would go. If you think this above is good land, then Victor will say come here Alexander: then our children will be content. That is the way we will make the treaty, my father." (Ibid., p. 309.) Although the Pend d'Oreille would not accept this proposal, Governor Stevens accepted it as applicable to the Flathead only. The compromise was embodied in the Flathead Treaty as Article XI.

Victor emerged from the Council with greatly increased prestige. By the terms of the treaty he had been made head chief of the Flathead Nation, comprising all the tribes party to the treaty. His compromise, which permitted the Flathead to remain in their beloved homeland until and unless a careful survey showed that the northern locality was better land, was popular with his people.

During the remainder of the period in which the Flathead were without a Mission, Victor made periodic visits to the Pend d'Oreille Mission to fulfill his religious obligations. A number of his tribesmen went with him. When St. Mary's Mission was reestablished in the fall of 1866, it was in answer to the request of Victor, whose faith had never faltered.

For the rest of his days Victor made his home in the Bitter-root Valley, and his people did not desert him for the reservation to the north. He opposed every effort of the Government to get him to go on the reservation, even after white settlers took up land in his valley. In 1872, after Victor's death, James A. Garfield stated that Victor had permitted, even invited, the first white settlers to live in the valley. (Ann. Rep. Comm. Ind. Aff., 1872, p. 110.) But by 1868 Victor complained to Major Owen of the white men who had located in the valley in defiance of the 1855 Treaty, which Victor said had set the area aside for the Flathead tribe. (Owen, 1927, vol. 2, p. 121.)

The Flathead Agent's report of 1869 describes the Flathead as:

> . . . the wealthiest, most industrious and frugal of these confederated tribes. Many of them rely wholly on the products of their farms for subsistence, but the majority live and subsist in the fall and winter in the buffalo country. [Ann. Rep. Comm. Ind. Aff., 1869, p. 297.]

Victor himself was unable to adjust to the life of a sedentary farmer. In the years following the treaty he continued to lead his people to the plains for buffalo in the tradition of prewhite contact days. Scattered references in Major Owen's Journal refer to Victor's leadership of the summer hunt of 1856; the winter hunt of 1860-61, which occupied 7 months; the winter hunt of 1861-62, during which the tribe was absent from the valley for 9 months and many horses and some men were lost (presumably as a result of enemy action); and the summer hunts of 1865, 1867, and 1869. (Owen, 1927, vol. I, pp. 136, 234, 253, 330; vol. 2, pp. 67, 138.)

In 1858 Victor was too ill to accompany the winter hunting party. He remained behind with three lodges of his people and was fed at Government expense. In mid-August, 1859, he was still an invalid, and Owen feared he would never recover his health. But he did. In the winter of 1867 Owen remarked at the amazing vitality of the old chief, whose hair was still black as coal and who could jump on a horse with as much agility as the youngest of his people. (Ibid., vol. I, pp. 184-185, 193; vol. 2, p. 42.)

Victor died of sickness while on the summer hunt near the Three Buttes in 1870. He is said to be buried in the cemetery of St. Mary's Mission at Stevensville, in the Bitterroot Valley.

George E. Ford, the Flathead Agent, paid tribute to Victor in his report of September I, 1870:

> Affairs are particularly critical just now, as the confederated nation is without a chief. The Indians had full confidence in Victor and would cheerfully act according to his advice, but I know of no one in the nation that is capable of filling his place with equal ability. [Ann. Rep. Comm. Ind. Aff., 1870, p. 195.]

Father De Smet's tribute to Victor stressed his piety. Captain Mullan remembered Victor's mildness and gentleness, bravery, generosity, and his many kindnesses to the members of his exploring expeditions. Mullan suggested that the Indian Department should erect a monument to Victor's memory "to commemorate his worth and acts, and at the same time to teach all Indians that their good deeds never die." A portrait of Victor, as a "representative of the religious element," was sought for a proposed new volume of Thomas L. McKenney's "History of the Indian Tribes of North America." (Chittenden and Richardson, 1905, vol. 4, pp. 1337-1341.) The little town of Victor, on the Bitterroot River, 12 miles north of Hamilton, Mont., bears the name of this noted chief.

Victor was head chief of the Flathead for nearly three decades during a particularly trying period in the history of that tribe. Although at times his leadership may have suffered from want of firmness in dealing with dissident elements, his sincere goodness, quiet courage, patience, and dogged determination won him wide respect in his later years. Victor's compromise offered at the Flathead Treaty Council was a statesmanlike action. His insistence on the right of his tribe to remain in the Bitterroot Valley won him the approval of his own people and the respect of Government officials. For 21 years after his death, his son and successor, Charlot, held stubbornly to Victor's policy of refusing to leave the Bitterroot Valley for the established reservation. Until the decade of the eighties this policy expressed the will of the majority of the members of the tribe.

MOISE, SECOND CHIEF OF THE FLATHEAD

Steit-tish-lutse-so or the Crawling Mountain
Known among the Americans as Moise
2nd chief of the Flatheads, a talented and worthy Indian

Moise (French for Moses) received his Christian name on baptism by Father De Smet at St. Mary's Mission on Easter, 1846. De Smet said that he was surnamed "Bravest of the Brave." (Chittenden and Richardson, 1905, vol. I, p. 305; vol. 2, p. 472.)

Moise told Lieutenant Mullan that he had been present in the Flathead camp in Ross' Hole when Lewis and Clark visited it in the fall of 1805. He said the explorers took what the Indians knew as the Southern Nez Perces' trail, following the Bitterroot River to its fork, after they left the Flathead village. (Report of Explorations, etc., 1860, vol. I, p. 325.)

Moise headed the Flathead delegation that went to meet Father De Smet at Fort Hall in 1841. He sent ahead his finest horse as a gift to the priest. After their meeting De Smet described Moise as "the handsomest Indian warrior of my acquaintance" who was "distinguished by his superior skill in horsemanship, and by a large red scarf, which he wore after the fashion of the Marshals of France." (Chittenden and Richardson, 1905, vol. I, p. 305.)

Moise remained a great favorite of Father De Smet, who called him his "adopted Indian brother" whose "exemplary conduct took pace with his renowned bravery and he was generally looked up to with esteem." As an example of Moise's moral refinement, De Smet recalled that on one occasion he and Moise had called upon a chief who had just flogged a visiting Nez Perce youth. Moise stripped off his buffalo robe, exposed his bare back, and called upon the chief to give him 25 lashes. When Father De Smet interposed, Moise explained, "Father, the Nez Perce here present was whipped because he talked foolishly to a girl. My thoughts are sometimes bewildering and vexing and I have prayed to drive them from my mind and heart." De Smet prevented the carrying out of this self-imposed punishment. (Ibid., vol. 4, pp. 1225-1226.)

De Smet told of Moise's calmness in encouraging his men before their successful battle with the Crow Indians east of the Rockies in the summer of 1846. "My friends," said Moise, "if it be the will of God, we shall conquer—if it be not his will, let us humbly submit to whatever it shall please his goodness to send us. Some of us must expect to fall in this contest: if there be any who are unprepared to die, let him retire; in the meantime let us keep Him constantly in mind." (Ibid., vol. 2, p. 576.)

In 1857 Father Menetrey named Moise among the four Flathead leaders who had never failed to follow the teachings of the missionaries after the closing of St. Mary's Mission. (Garraghan, 1938, vol. 2, p. 388.) Moise was one of the Flathead chiefs who journeyed to St. Ignatius to fulfill his religious duties in that year. (Chittenden and Richardson, 1905, vol. 4, p. 1240.) After his visit to the Flathead in 1859 De Smet termed Moise one of the greatest chieftains of the tribe, in whom real piety and true valor at war were united. (Ibid., vol. 2, p. 766.)

At the Flathead Treaty Council, Moise remained silent until he was asked to sign the treaty. He refused to sign. Then he launched a bitter denunciation of the treaty. He claimed the Flathead leaders would not have come to the council at all if Lieutenant Mullan had not assured them there would be "no talk of land," and that its purpose would be to offer help to the Flathead in their struggle against the Blackfoot. He refused to consider cession of any Flathead land. He had no faith in Governor Stevens' promise to make peace with the Blackfoot. Although Moise was the only Flathead leader to express these ideas at the Council, and the only one to refuse to sign the treaty, it is possible he voiced the sentiments of a large segment of Flathead opinion. In the course of his remarks Moise also revealed his independence of Victor. When asked directly if Victor, who had already signed the treaty, was not his head chief, Moise replied bluntly, "Yes, but I never listen to him." (Partoll, 1938, p. 311.)

Although Moise attended the Blackfoot Treaty Council that fall, and signed the treaty, he took no speaking part in the proceedings.

Scattered references to Moise's activities in the years following the treaties appear in Major Owen's Journal: In early April, 1857, Moise sought Owen's assistance to dissuade some of the young warriors from going to war against the Bannock and Shoshoni. During Victor's prolonged illness in 1858 Moise and Ambrose led the Flathead on their winter buffalo hunt. In March 1861 Moise brought up the rear of the Flathead camp on its return from hunting on the plains. In the winter hunt of 1862-63 he was a leader. On May 18, 1865, Moise started out with Victor and the Flathead party for the summer hunt east of the mountains but changed his mind and returned the next day in order to care for his growing crops. This is the only indication that any Flathead chief of the period was sufficiently interested in farming to permit it to interfere with his going to hunt buffalo. Apparently, even in this case, Moise had some difficulty reaching a decision in favor of tending his crops. (Owen, 1927, vol. I, pp. 160, 190, 234, 277, 330.)

Moise died in March 1868, following a tedious year of sickness. Modern Flathead believe that he was buried in the Bitterroot Valley. At the time of his death Moise must have been over 70 years of age. Ambrose became his successor as second chief of the tribe. (Ibid., vol. 2, p. 95.) Moise, the headquarters of the National Bison Range, near Dixon, Mont., was named after Antoine Moise, a son, who was also a prominent Flathead leader.

Moise was a leader who combined the Christian virtues with the tough qualities necessary for survival on the northwestern Indian frontier in his time. He was honest, God-fearing, brave in war, and both independent and frankly outspoken in council. Later events proved that in his distrust of the possibility for a lasting peace with the Blackfoot, Moise possessed a keen and realistic insight into the military problems of the region.

AMBROSE, SUCCESSOR TO MOISE AS FLATHEAD SECOND CHIEF

Ambrose (in baptism)
Shil-che-lum-e-la, or Five Crows
A chief of the Flatheads, mentioned many times in the "Oregon Missions," for his bravery and generosity.

Father De Smet wrote Ambrose's Indian name "Sechelmeld." (Chittenden and Richardson, 1905, vol. I, p. 320.) Father Palladino considered "Amelo or Ambrose" one of the notable men of the Flathead tribe. (Palladino, 1894, p. 63.) He is remembered by the modern Flathead by the names "Amelo" and "Five Crows."

In a battle with the Blackfoot in 1840 Ambrose counted coup by permitting an armed Blackfoot, who had mistaken him for one of his own tribe, to ride double with him, then wresting the enemy warrior's gun from him and killing him. (Chittenden and Richardson, 1905, vol. I, p. 320. The editors state that Ambrose's own drawing of this action is among Father De Smet's papers.)

Ambrose (in baptism)

The Catholic missionaries considered Ambrose one of the Flathead leaders who remained loyal to their cause after the abandonment of the Mission. (Menetrey *in* Garraghan, 1938, vol. 2, p. 388; Chittenden and Richardson, 1905, vol. 2, p. 766.) Twice in 1857 he accompanied Victor to St. Ignatius to fulfill his religious obligations. Father Hoecken credited Ambrose with having played an influential part in a notable amelioration in the whole Flathead Nation in that year. Ambrose had "convened several assemblages, in order to arrange and pay off old debts, to repair wrongs, etc." (Chittenden and Richardson, vol. 4, p. 1240.)

During the Flathead Treaty Council, Ambrose revealed that Victor had refused Alexander's offer to move onto a reservation in the Bitterroot Valley, which resulted in Governor Stevens' relentless attack upon Victor. Ambrose quickly came to Victor's defense and attempted to restore calm to the proceedings by remarking, "I say to the white chief, don't get angry, maybe it will come out all right. Maybe all the people have a great many minds. Maybe they will come all right. See my chiefs are now holding down their heads thinking." (Partoll, 1938, p. 305.)

Ambrose signed both the Flathead and Blackfoot Treaties. A year after he signed the Blackfoot "treaty of peace," his son, Louis, was killed by the Gros Ventres, a party to that treaty. (Chittenden and Richardson, 1905, vol. 4, p. 1248.)

Through the late fifties and sixties Ambrose continued to go on buffalo hunts with his tribe. During Victor's illness in 1858 he shared with Moise the leadership of the Flathead hunting camp. Again in 1863 Ambrose and Moise led the Flathead hunting camp on the Musselshell River. After the death of Moise, in the spring of 1868, Ambrose succeeded to the office of second chief of the Flathead. (Owen, 1927, vol. I, pp. 190, 277; vol. 2, p. 101.)

The date of Ambrose's death is not recorded. However, we may assume that he died sometime between the end of March 1869 (when he was last mentioned by Owen, 1927, vol. 2, p. 133), and August 1872, at which time Arlee was recognized as second chief of the Flathead. (Ann. Rep. Comm. Ind. Aff., 1873, p. 251.)

As a leader, Ambrose exhibited admirable qualities of faith, courage, honesty, patience, and common sense. He showed remarkable coolness in battle and at the Flathead Treaty Council. His words of caution, offered at a crucial point in the Council proceedings, when tempers were aroused, helped to prevent a complete breakdown in negotiations.

ADOLPHE, A FLATHEAD CHIEF

Adolphe (in baptism)
A chief among the Flatheads, noted for his independence and good sense. Not much liked because he never fails to reprimand any of his tribe who may deserve it

Pierre Pichette said Adolphe's Indian name was "Wears his Hair in Small Twists," and that he was said to have used one of these twists to spank children who misbehaved. Adolphe's peculiar hair-dress is well illustrated in Sohon's portrait.

Martina Siwahsah remembered Adolphe as a powerful medicine man. She said she was present on a winter hunt on the plains when the snow was so deep the horses were dying of starvation. One evening the people heard someone singing. It was Adolphe making his medicine to bring a chinook. In the morning the chinook struck, and before evening the snow was all gone.

Peter Ronan said that Adolphe used to lead the Flathead against their enemies as their war chief. In a battle with the Gros Ventres

Adolphe - (in baptism)

about the year 1840 Adolphe and Arlee led the Flathead to a decisive victory. About half the Gros Ventres force, estimated at 100 warriors, were killed. (Ronan, 1890, pp. 76-78.)

The missionaries considered Adolphe one of the Flathead leaders who retained their faith and loyalty after the closure of St. Mary's Mission in 1850. (Menetrey *in* Garraghan, 1938, vol. 2, p. 338: Chittenden and Richardson, 1905, vol. 2, p. 766.) He journeyed to St. Ignatius with Victor in 1857, to fulfill his religious obligations. (Chittenden and Richardson, 1905, vol. 4, p. 1240.)

Governor Stevens mentioned Adolphe among the principal men of the tribe whom he met on his first visit to the Flathead at Fort Owen, October 1, 1853. (Report of Explorations, etc., 1860, vol. 12, pt. I, p. 125.) Adolphe signed both the Flathead and Blackfoot Treaties of 1855, but took no other part in the proceedings. "Adolphus Kwiikweschape, or Red Feather, chief of the Flatheads" was one of the group of chiefs of the mountain tribes who accompanied Father De Smet to Fort Vancouver in the spring of 1859 to renew the treaty of peace with the Commanding General and Superintendent of Indian Affairs. (Chittenden and Richardson, 1905, vol. 2, p. 766.)

When James A. Garfield, Commissioner for the Removal of the Flathead tribe of Indians from the Bitterroot Valley to the Jocko Reservation, met the chiefs of the tribe near Fort Owen in 1872, Adolphe, as third chief of the Flathead, was one of the tribal representatives. On August 27, 1872, he signed the agreement drawn up by Garfield providing for the removal of the Flathead to the reservation. Nevertheless, he joined with head chief Charlot in refusing to leave the Bitterroot Valley. Three years later Agent Medary removed Adolphe's name from the Government payroll, because he had "failed in every particular" to comply with the provisions of the agreement. (Ann. Rep. Comm. Ind. Aff., 1872, pp. 109, 114-115; 1875, p. 305.)

Adolphe marshaled and led the young warriors at the council held at the Flathead Agency September 2, 1882, to negotiate a right-of-way for the Northern Pacific Railway. Apparently before that date he had removed from the Bitterroot Valley to the reservation. Adolphe died at the Agency in 1887, at an assumed age of 78 years. (Ronan, 1890, p.76.)

Insula — or Red feat.

Michelle (in baptism)

INSULA, A FLATHEAD CHIEF

Insula—or Red Feather
Michelle (in baptism)
A Flathead chief; according to Father De Smet "a great and brave
warrior." He is noted for his piety, and officiates at the burial of the
dead. He is quite an old man, nearly seventy.

Michael Insula (sometimes rendered Ensyla or Insala), Red
Feather, was also known as "The Little Chief," because of his small
stature. (Chittenden and Richardson, 1905, vol. 4, p. 1231.) Pierre

Pichette thought Insula was not a name of Flathead origin. According to Duncan McDonald, he was half Nez Perce and half Flathead, and lived part time with the Flathead and the remainder of the time with the Pend d'Oreille. (Owen, 1927, vol. I, p. 236, footnote.) De Smet stated (1841) that the Nez Perce had offered Insula the position of head chief of their tribe. He refused the honor saying, "By the will of the Great Master of Life I was born among the Flatheads, and if such be his will, among the Flatheads I am determined to die." (Chittenden and Richardson, 1905, vol. I, p. 323.)

In the summer of 1835 Insula journeyed to the Green River rendezvous of the fur traders, where in company with a group of Nez Perce, he met the Protestant missionaries, Rev. Samuel Parker and Dr. Marcus Whitman. The Reverend Parker recorded his conversation thus:

> Next rose Insala, the most influential chief among the Flathead nation, and said, "he had heard that a man near to God was coming to visit them, and he, with some of his people, together with some white men, went out three days' journey to meet him, but failed of finding the caravan. A war party of Crow Indians came upon them in the night, and after a short battle, though no lives were lost, they took away some of their horses, and one from him which he greatly loved, but now he forgets all, his heart is made so glad to see a man close to God." [Parker, 1844, pp. 81-82.]

Many years later Father Palladino explained that Insula was not satisfied with the appearance or the message of Parker and Whitman. He observed that they wore neither black gowns nor crosses, that they married, and did not have the great prayer, and that therefore these were not the priests of whom the Iroquois had told him. Consequently, he did not encourage them to go to the Flathead country. (Palladino, 1894, pp. 16-17.)

Insula was a great favorite of the Catholic missionaries. He was one of the party of 30 warriors who accompanied Father De Smet as far as Fort Alexander on the Yellowstone in the country of the enemy Crow Indians on De Smet's return eastward in 1840. (Chittenden and Richardson, 1905, vol. I, pp. 266-267.) In 1841 De Smet termed Insula "the most influential of the Flathead chiefs," who "as a Christian or a warrior, might stand a comparison with the most renowned character of ancient chivalry." (Ibid., p. 324.)

Father Adrian Hoecken also had a marked personal regard for Insula. In the fall of 1855 he wrote De Smet of Insula's great bravery, tender piety, and gentle manners, and added that he had "preserved all his first fervor of devotion." Again in the spring of 1857 he wrote of Insula as "always equally good, equally happy, a fervent Christian, who is daily advancing in virtue and in perfection." He added that Insula had taught his young son, Louis Michael, to call the priest papa. (Ibid., vol. 4, p. 1245.)

Father Hoecken wrote that Insula "is well known and much beloved by the whites, who have occasion to deal with him, as a man of sound judgment, strict integrity, and one on whose fidelity they can implicitly rely." The priest called Insula "a keen discerner of the characters of men" who "loved to speak of those white men who were distinguished for their fine qualities." Insula adopted Col. Robert Campbell of St. Louis and Maj. Thomas Fitzpatrick as brothers. Colonel Campbell reciprocated by sending him a fine present in the spring of 1857. (Ibid., pp. 1232, 1245.)

Of Insula's numerous deeds of heroism, Father De Smet cited but two, both of which occurred before 1841. On one occasion Insula "sustained the assaults of a whole village" of the enemy. On another, a party of Bannock, estimated at 200, who had visited Insula's camp and observed the small number of the Flathead, returned to attack the Flathead the next night. Advised of their intentions, Insula assembled his warriors to meet the attack. The small Flathead force killed nine of the enemy before Insula, in the heat of the pursuit, recalled that it was Sunday and ordered his warriors back to camp for prayer. (Ibid., vol. 1, pp. 322-324, 365-366.)

According to Duncan McDonald, Insula was killed by Cree and Assiniboine on Milk River in October 1860. At that time the old man was living with the Kutenai and Pend d'Oreille. (Owen, 1927, vol. 1, p. 236, footnote.)

Little Insula appears to have possessed the most appealing personality among the Flathead leaders of his time. Not only was he very popular with the Indians of his own and friendly tribes, but he also proved adept at winning and holding the friendship of influential white men. Apparently he found subtle flattery, such as teaching his son to call the priest papa and adopting important white men as brothers, helpful in cementing these friendships. An ardent Catholic and a courageous warrior, he epitomized the missionaries' ideal of the Christian soldier.

BEAR TRACK, FLATHEAD CHIEF AND MEDICINE MAN

Soey-te-sum-'hi or Bear Track.
A Chief, and one of the very few pure Flathead Indians in the tribe. He is said to be a very brave and daring man, and is certainly one of the best looking men in the tribe, decision is written in every line of his countenance.

Soey-te-sum-'hi, or Bear Track.

Bear Track spoke at the Flathead Treaty Council on July 13, 1855, after Victor's refusal to accept Alexander's offer to move to the Bitterroot Valley. He made no reference to Victor's action. He expressed his own willingness to make a treaty but emphasized the poverty of his people and his opinion that the area around St. Ignatius Mission was not large enough for the proposed reservation. Bear Track signed both the Flathead and Blackfoot Treaties. (Partoll, 1938, p. 306.)

Bear Track was famous as a medicine man. He was the maternal grandfather of Martina Siwahsah, who recalled some of Bear Track's remarkable feats. One spring the Indians were camped north of Hamilton in the Bitterroot Valley. A man and his wife went out hunting in the mountains. While his wife remained in the hunting camp, the man went on alone after game. She waited 3 days, but he did not return. Then she went back to the tribe and told Bear Track of her husband's disappearance. He sang, made his medicine, and said, "All I can see is the horse your husband was riding tied to a tree. I don't see the rider." He described the locality where he saw the horse. Men went to that place. They found the horse tied where Bear Track had indicated and the dead body of the hunter nearby. Apparently he had made a fire, gone to sleep, and a log rolled over and killed him.

Another time the people were hunting buffalo and could find none. Bear Track told the people to erect a long tent. He made his medicine, then told the people, "My power I received from a white buffalo calf. The buffalo are coming, and that calf will be in the lead." Next day a herd of buffalo appeared led by a white calf.

Teit also has reported Bear Track's power to find lost people and to bring the buffalo when they could not be found. He also stated that Bear Track had the power to foresee the approach of parties of enemy horse thieves and to warn his people in advance, as well as the power to foretell the results of battles. (Teit, 1930, pp. 384-385.) Turney-High found that no Flathead shamans were more highly respected than those who possessed such powers. (Turney-High, 1937, p. 29.)

Probably Bear Track was the most successful and most famous medicine man of his day among the Flathead. That he is not mentioned in the voluminous correspondence of the missionaries is understandable. It is unlikely that this medicine man of the traditional school looked with much favor upon the "magic" of the whites. Never-

90

theless, Martina Siwahsah said Bear Track was baptized and given the Christian name of "Alexander."

She said that Bear Track was married four times. He fathered 10 children. He lived to be a very old man, became blind, and died of sickness during the 1880's. Teit dated Bear Track's death about 1880, at over 90 years of age. (Teit, 1930, p. 384.)

PELCHIMO, A FLATHEAD CHIEF

Koilt-koi-imp-ty (Indian name)
Spoken of by Father De Smet as "Pelchimo", (by which name he is generally known,) as a good and brave Indian. He is a great favorite of all the whites who know him, for his honesty and good sense.

The modern Flathead remember him by both his Indian name and by the name "Palchina." They could not translate his Indian name exactly, because it is an obsolete form, referring to a blanket with some black on it.

Pelchimo was a brother of one of the Indians of the ill-fated third deputation (1837), the members of which were killed by the Sioux while en route to St. Louis to seek a priest. (Chittenden and Richardson, 1905, vol. 1, p. 292; Palladino, 1894, p. 30.) As "Palchinah" he signed the Blackfoot Treaty in the fall of 1855. His name does not appear among the signers of the Flathead Treaty.

Pelchimo was one of the heroes in the battle with the Blackfoot in 1840, in which Ambrose also distinguished himself. In this battle the Flathead, though greatly outnumbered, withstood their opponents for 5 days and finally forced them to retreat, leaving many killed and wounded on the battlefield. The Flathead lost but a single man, who died of wounds received in the battle. Pelchimo won honors in this fight by saving the Flathead horses from capture by the enemy. (Chittenden and Richardson, 1905, vol. 1, pp. 319-320.)

Pelchimo was a great friend of Major Owen. Owen frequently referred to him as "Palchina" in his Journals. In 1851 he accompanied Owen to Fort Loring on Snake River. They traveled together to The Dalles in the spring of 1855, and to Fort Benton in the summer of 1858. (Owen, 1927, vol. 1, p. 28-35.)

Hoelt-koi-imta-ty (Indian man)

Owen considered Palchina the best veterinary in the region, and employed him to doctor his own favorite horses. He also had Palchina break his horses and permitted him to use the horses during the summer buffalo hunt in return for "getting them gentle." (Ibid., pp. 127-128.)

On April 4, 1863, Owen received a report that 70 horses had been stolen from Palchina's camp while en route home from the buffalo hunt on the plains. Two days later he was informed that Palchina had been killed by the party of Bannock horse thieves from whom Palchina sought to recover his stolen property. On hearing of Palchina's death, Owen paid high tribute to the man's character as one of the best Indians, brave when danger called, inoffensive but firm and exacting in his rights. (Ibid., pp. 278-279.)

The written record appears to emphasize Pelchimo's prowess in the traditional men's occupations of the Flathead. He was a courageous fighter, a clever hunter, and a skilled trainer of horses. His talents as a horse doctor must have given him considerable prestige as a medicine man among the conservative members of his tribe. He was not mentioned by the missionaries among the Flathead leaders who remained staunchly loyal to their cause after the closure of St. Mary's Mission in 1850. Nevertheless, Sohon's testimony as to his good character is confirmed by the writings of Father De Smet and Major Owen.

THUNDER, A FLATHEAD LEADER

Til-til-la or Thunder
Said to be one of the bravest of the Flathead Indians.

Father Palladino considered "Phidel Teltella, or Thunder," one of the notable men of the Flathead tribe. (Palladino, 1894, p. 63.) As "Thunder" he signed both the Flathead and Blackfoot Treaties in 1855, but he took no speaking part in the proceedings.

When disease in epidemic proportions raged in the Flathead camp in the summer of 1856, "Fidelis Teltilla" asked Father Menetrey to

see his son who was dangerously ill. In the next year he accompanied Victor to St. Ignatius Mission to fulfill his religious duties. (Chittenden and Richardson, 1905, vol. 4, pp. 1239-1240.) Doubtless, the name "Fidelis" was given him by the missionaries in reference to his steadfastness in the Christian faith.

The modern Flathead say that Thunder died in the Bitterroot Valley before 1891.

PACHA, A FLATHEAD LEADER

Pacha
One of the chief men of the Flatheads—He is quite an old man.
(Indian Name) Quill-Quill-che-koil-pent.

Very little is known about this man. He was one of the principal men of the Flathead who met Governor Stevens at Fort Owen in the fall of 1853, on Stevens' first visit to the tribe. (Report of Explorations, etc., 1860, vol. 12, pt. 2, p. 125.) He may have been the Indian who signed the Flathead Treaty under the name of "Pah-soh." Doubtless he died within a few years after the treaty.

He was not remembered by any of the elderly Flathead questioned by the writer in 1947. They translated his Indian name, "Red Plume."

GUSTAVUS SOHON'S PORTRAITS OF UPPER PEND D'OREILLE LEADERS

The eight pencil portraits of Upper Pend d'Oreille leaders drawn by Gustavus Sohon in the spring of 1854 include likenesses of the three most important chiefs of the tribe during the period 1848-1890. These three, Alexander, Big Canoe, and Michelle, were signers of both the Flathead and Blackfoot Treaties of 1855. Bonaparte, a minor chief, is also included. The remaining four portraits of Choits-Kan, Pierre Nu-ah-ute-se, Louis Ramo, and Broken Leg (Kousheene), represent men of less standing in the tribe about whom no additional biographical information is available.

ALEXANDER, HEAD CHIEF OF THE UPPER PEND D'OREILLE

Alexander (English Name)
Tum-cle-hot-cut-se (Indian name)
Alexander the principal chief of the Pends-d-oreilles is not a Pend-d-Oreille proper but descended on the father's side from the Snake Indians and on the mother's from the Pends-d-Oreilles. He was made "First Chief" by the Pends-d-oreilles themselves and by the Jesuit Priests in 1848. He is noted for his high-toned, sterling and noble traits of character. He is a brave man. When a party of his tribe had stolen horses from Fort Benton on the Missouri in 1853, he started with only five of his men and carried them back, passing through the whole camp of the Blackfeet Indians, then most deadly enemies. He still rules the Pends-d-oreille tribe of Indians and is 45 years old.

Le Sohon
April 21st 1854.

Alexander (English name.)
Tun-cle-hot-cut-se (Indian name).

Flathead Reservation Indians have translated Alexander's Indian name as "No Horses."

In addition to the return of the stolen horses, cited by Sohon above, other known exploits of Alexander testify to his courage. As a young man he volunteered to go alone to a trading post in the country of the hostile Crow Indians to obtain powder and lead which was badly needed by his tribe. Again, in the spring of 1856, after he had accompanied Major Owen to Fort Benton to obtain ammunition for his people, Alexander and two of his men set out alone on the return trip through the country of their Blackfoot enemies, killed nine buffalo on the plains, and rejoined Owen at the eastern base of the Rockies. (Ronan, 1890, pp. 73-76; Owen, 1927, vol. 1, pp. 118-121.)

Alexander succeeded Joseph as chief of his tribe. (Ronan, 1890, p. 73.) At the Flathead Treaty Council, he claimed to be chief of the Lower Pend d'Oreille as well. Governor Stevens promptly denied Alexander's claim to leadership of the Lower Pend d'Oreille or his right to speak for that group at the Council. (Partoll, 1938, pp. 299-300.)

In the Flathead Treaty Council, Alexander clashed with Victor, the Flathead head chief, over the location of the reservation for the combined Flathead-Pend d'Oreille-Kutenai tribes. He readily agreed to Governor Stevens' proposal to place these tribes on one reservation, but he strongly favored the northern or Flathead Valley location. He argued that wild fruits and berries were plentiful there, that his crops grew well there, that it was a larger area than the Bitterroot Valley, and that the Kutenai and Lower Pend d'Oreille as well as his own people would prefer the northern location. When it became apparent that Victor would not accept this proposal, Alexander magnanimously went to Victor and offered to move to the Bitterroot Valley. But when Victor did not accept this offer immediately, Alexander withdrew it. Later Alexander offered to acknowledge Victor as his chief if Victor would accept the northern reservation. Again Victor was deaf to Alexander's proposal. Subsequently, Alexander refused Victor's compromise proposal to abide by the Government's decision as to the better location following a survey of the resources of both areas. He no longer would consider any reservation site but the northern one.

The Treaty, as finally drawn up and signed, secured to the Upper Pend d'Oreille their right to residence on a reservation in their traditional homeland. The Flathead Treaty, which was to plague Victor the rest of his life, was a complete victory of Alexander.

At the Blackfoot Treaty Council in October 1855 Alexander did not hesitate to express his dissatisfaction with both the location and the small size of the area proposed by the Commissioners as a buffalo-hunting ground for the western tribes. They had set aside a relatively limited tract east of the Rockies, west of the Crow territory, and south of the Musselshell River, as a common hunting ground in which the Blackfoot and the tribes from west of the mountains might hunt, but in which none of the tribes might establish permanent villages. Alexander vigorously championed the right of his people to hunt on the plains of present Montana, in the area the Commissioners wished to reserve to the Blackfoot. Alexander based his argument soundly on the traditional use of the area by his people, saying

> A long time ago our people, our ancestors belonged in this country. The country around the Three Buttes. We had many people on this side of the mountains.... A long time ago our people used to hunt about the Three Buttes and the Blackfeet lived far north. When my Father was living he told me that was an old road for our people.

Alexander demanded to know why his people could not continue to cross the Rockies by the northern passes (referring probably to the Cut Bank and Marias passes). Although Little Dog, a prominent Piegan chief, was impressed by Alexander's argument, the Commissioners remained firm in their decision that the country north of the Musselshell should be reserved for the Blackfoot tribes. The Treaty as written and signed by Alexander as well as the other Pend d'Oreille chiefs, gave the western Indians no right to hunt in the area reserved for the Blackfoot. (Partoll, 1937, pp. 7-10.)

Nevertheless, Alexander continued to hunt there. In 1860 he led his people on their winter hunt over the Rockies and across the plains of the Blackfoot country until they discovered buffalo on Milk River. After the people had thanked God for the prospect of a successful hunt, and secured their best horses for the morrow's chase, they retired for the night. While they slept, a large war party of Assiniboine and Cree Indians on foot surrounded the camp. An hour before dawn they launched a surprise attack, killed 20 of the Pend d'Oreille and wounded 25 more (5 of whom later died of their wounds). The enemy stole 290 Pend d'Oreille horses and forced the defeated camp to abandon most of their equipment, provisions, and clothing on the battlefield. Alexander led his beaten people on the 400-mile retreat homeward across the plains. Women with their children on their backs were forced to make the entire journey on foot. Major Owen met the party on its return to the Jocko Reservation. He found Alexander thirsting for revenge. Not only had his people suffered a humiliating defeat, but Alexander's son, a promising young man of 20 years of age, had been among those killed. Alexander had seen his son's scalped and mutilated body. He longed to return to the sleeping place of his son and people and to avenge their loss. (Owen, 1927, vol. 2, pp. 234-235, 239, 262.)

Alexander was deeply concerned with the problem of disciplining his people. In his first recorded speech at the Flathead Treaty Council he spoke frankly of his difficulties in managing his unruly young people. He believed that good example alone would not "make them go straight." Yet he feared the severity of the white man's laws. (Partoll, 1938, pp. 289-290.) When Alexander accompanied Father De Smet to Fort Vancouver in the spring of 1859, he showed little interest in the white man's mechanical inventions and industrial plants he saw in the principal towns of Oregon and Washington. He was much interested in the Portland prison and the severe methods of punishment of criminals he observed there. Immediately on his return to the reservation, Alexander assembled his people. He told them of the wonders of the white man's civilization, placing particular emphasis upon the white man's severe methods of criminal punishment, and concluded:

> We have neither chains nor prisons, and for want of them, no doubt, a great number of us are wicked and have deaf ears. As chief, I am determined to do my duty; I shall take a whip to punish the wicked; let all those who have been guilty of any misdemeanor present themselves. I am ready.

The outcome of the affair was as follows:

> The known guilty parties were called upon by name, many presented themselves of their own accord, and all received a proportionate correction. The whole affair terminated in a general rejoicing and feast. [Chittenden and Richardson, 1905, vol. 2, pp. 767-768.]

Alexander was a close friend of the Jesuit Missionaries. He often accompanied Father De Smet on his travels in the Rocky Mountain region. Father Hoecken credited Alexander with having selected the site for St. Ignatius Mission on its removal eastward in the fall of 1854. At the Flathead Treaty Council, Alexander declared, "The priest instructs me and this people here. I am very well content with the priest." At one point in the controversy over the location of the reservation, Alexander stated that he would agree to leave the area around the Mission and go on a reservation in the Bitterroot Valley if Governor Stevens would say that he could not go to heaven at his own place. His strong attachment to the Mission influenced his ultimate refusal to accept the southern reservation proposed by Governor Stevens. (Ibid., vol. 4, p. 1232; Partoll, 1938, pp. 290, 300.)

Alexander died about the year 1868. (Teit, 1930, p. 377.) Thus he served as head chief of the Upper Pend d'Oreille for two decades. His leadership was courageous, aggressive, strict, and apparently just. There is no record of Alexander's position ever having been seriously challenged by a rival leader of the tribe. His chieftaincy was marked by continued friendship with the whites and sporadic warfare with the plains tribes. Alexander was an economic conservative. At the time of his death the Upper Pend d'Oreille still made periodic hunting excursions to the plains for buffalo.

MICHELLE, SUCCESSOR TO ALEXANDER AS UPPER PEND D'OREILLE HEAD CHIEF

Whe-whitth-schay (Indian name)
Michelle (English name)
Is noted for his upright and manly conduct, he was well thought of among the Jesuit Priests who gave him the name Michelle. He is remarkable for his generosity, which is the significance of his name.

Michelle's Indian name means "Plenty of Grizzly Bear." He was a minor chief of the tribe when Alexander died, and was elected head chief after two others, Andre and Pierre, declined the office. (Teit, 1930, p. 377.) He was probably one of the Michelles who signed the Flathead Treaty and possibly the Michelle who signed the Blackfoot Treaty in 1855. He took no speaking part in either Council. As Pend d'Oreille head chief he represented the tribe in the Council to negotiate for the right-of-way of the Northern Pacific Railway on the reservation, September 2,

Whe - whitils - schay.

1882, and at the meeting with members of the subcommittee of the United States Senate appointed to visit the Indian tribes of northern Montana on September 7, 1882. (Ronan, 1890, pp. 54, 76.)

In his Annual Report of September 1874 Peter Whaley, the Flathead Agent, recommended that Michelle should be replaced by Andre, second chief of the tribe. The Agent pointed out that on their buffalo hunts east of the mountains the Pend d'Oreille were in the habit of stealing horses from friends and foes alike and refused to return the animals to their proper owners. Michelle, who at the time was physically unable to accompany his people on their hunts, was powerless to prevent the thefts or to compel restitution. Andre, on the other hand, had the confidence of his people and was the real leader of the tribe. (Ann. Rep. Comm. Ind. Aff., 1874, pp. 262-263.) The new Flathead Agent in 1875 reported that Andre was "chief in all but drawing a salary from the government." (Ibid., 1875, p. 304.) Agent Peter Ronan investigated the cause of the dissension in 1877. He found Michelle a "good-meaning" man who had to a large extent lost contact with his people. Michelle lived at the Agency while his people were located near St. Ignatius Mission some 20 miles away. When decisions needed to be made, Andre, who lived with the tribe, generally made them. If a case was later taken to Michelle, he generally reversed Andre's decision, causing further dissatisfaction. Michelle seemed well aware of the fact that he had lost contact with his people and considered moving back to live among them in order to regain his lost influence. (Ibid., 1877, p. 136.)

Michelle's popularity was not increased by his severe punishments. He whipped female adulterers, common among his people, so severely as to cause the deaths of some women. Agent Medary found it necessary to prevail upon Michelle to resort to milder punishment. (Ibid., 1876, p. 89.)

In spite of the dissatisfaction of many of his people, the opposition of Andre, and the recommendation of at least one Agent that he be deposed, Michelle continued in the position of head chief. He won the respect of Agent Ronan during the Nez Perce War of 1877. Fearing that the Agency Indians might join their old allies, Ronan prepared to remove his wife and children from danger. Michelle went to the Agent and pledged that his warriors would protect Ronan's family from harm. The Pend d'Oreille remained friendly. (Clark, 1885, p. 301.)

A few years earlier, Michelle's friendship for the whites had been put to a severe test. His son had been accused of the murder of a white miner. Although the son swore his innocence, Michelle told him he could not be saved, or his death avenged, except by war with the whites, and asked the young man to sacrifice his life for the good of his people. The youth was hung by enraged whites. (Ibid.)

Michelle helped to set an example for his people in agriculture. In 1885 he had 160 acres under fence, producing 250 bushels of wheat and oats. In the spring of 1887 he purchased young fruit trees for his land 16 miles north of the Mission. (Ann. Rep. Comm. Ind. Aff., 1885, p. 127; 1887, p. 138.)

Michelle died at his home, near the present town of Ronan, about 1890. He is said to have been buried in the cemetery at St. Ignatius Mission.

Although he possessed admirable personal qualities, as a leader of his people Michelle proved a rather ineffective successor to the active and aggressive Alexander.

BIG CANOE, SECOND CHIEF OF THE UPPER PEND D'OREILLE

In-er-cult-say
Known as the "Big Canoe."
Full-blooded Pend d'Oreille, second chief—Rather a dark Indian,
about 55 or 60 years old.

Big Canoe is said to have been born in 1799. (Handbook of American Indians, etc., 1910, pt. 1, p. 146.) At the Flathead Treaty Council, he made a point of the fact that his aunt told him he was "pure Pend d' Oreille." (Partoll, 1938, p. 293.) Pierre Pichette translates his Indian name, "Rotted Under the Belt," which probably refers to a rotten scalp carried under the belt as a trophy.

Peter Ronan stated that Big Canoe "was considered by the Indians to be one of the greatest war chiefs the tribe of the Pend d'Orielle ever had," and that "stories of battles led by him against Indian foes would fill a volume." (Ronan, 1890, p. 73.) Unfortunately, none of those deeds have been recorded in the literature.

At the Flathead Treaty Council in 1855 Big Canoe delivered a lengthy speech. He could not understand why discussion at the Council involved the problem of Indian land. To his mind no real land problem existed. The whites and Indians could live peaceably side by side. He pointed with pride to the fact that his people had never spilt blood of the white man. Why then should there be a treaty? He attributed the continued friendship between his people and the whites to the fact that white traders had furnished guns and ammunition to repel their powerful enemies, and for this his people continued to be grateful. However, he resented the fact that the whites also traded these things to the

Blackfoot who used their weapons against whites as well as Indians. He referred to Governor Stevens' promise to put an end to Blackfoot depredations. He pointed out that since the Blackfoot promised peace in 1853, they had broken it many times. They had stolen one of his horses the previous winter, and his own daughter had been set afoot when they stole two horses that very spring. He had kept his promise not to retaliate against the Blackfoot, not because he was afraid of them, but because the white man had asked him to keep the peace. To Big Canoe this matter of Blackfoot hostility was the only important problem for discussion at the Council.

Governor Stevens made no direct reply to Big Canoe. He guided the discussion back to the subject of the choice of a reservation for the Indians. Big Canoe remained silent through the remainder of the Council. At its conclusion he signed the Treaty. (Partoll, 1938, pp. 291-294.)

At the Blackfoot Treaty Council, Big Canoe spoke briefly in support of Alexander's claim of the right of the Pend d'Oreille to hunt buffalo on the plains north of the Musselshell. He spoke bluntly, "I am glad now we are together. I thought our roads would be all over this country. Now you tell us different. Supposing we do stick together, and do make a peace.... Now you tell me not to step over that way. I had a mind to go there." Later he concurred in the expressed desire for peace of the Piegan chief, Lame Bull, saying "Don't let your war parties hide from me. Let them come to our camps as friends." (Ibid., 1937, p. 8.)

Big Canoe was a strong character. Although a war leader, he had a sincere desire for peace. To his mind peace seemed to promise unrestricted freedom of movement. He could not reconcile his idea of peaceful relationships with the whites and other Indians with the talk of separate tribal hunting grounds and restricted reservations that was current at the Councils.

Big Canoe died at the Flathead Agency in 1882 at the advanced age of 83. He was buried in the Indian Cemetery at St. Ignatius Mission (Ronan, 1890, p. 72).

BONAPARTE, A PEND D'OREILLE CHIEF

Bonaparte (English name)
Kols-seese-Kol-lay (Indian name)
Bonaparte a Pend-d-oreille chief is noted for his generosity and benevolence to his tribe and especially to those who are poor or needy. He is rich in horses and cattle and a person is never known to be in need without his assisting him and relieving his wants. He is a man of thirty-five years of age.

Pierre Pichette said that Bonaparte's Indian name was an obsolete form which he was unable to translate. Apparently he was a minor chief in 1855, for his name is not signed to either the Flathead or Blackfoot Treaties.

Major Owen, in May 1856, told of a half-breed named Bonaparte who attempted to arrange a horse race between his prized mount and a Nez Perce race horse. However, Bonaparte's horse, which he had obtained from the Spokan country 2 years before in exchange for six

Bonaparte (English name.)
Kols-seeee-Kol-lay/ Indian name.

horses, bore such a reputation for speed that its owner could get no other Indians to race against it. (Owen, 1927, vol. 1, pp. 125-126.)

Indians living on the Flathead Reservation today say that Bonaparte died in the 1870's.

CHOITS-KAN

Choits-Kan (Indian Name)
Choits-Kan, a Pend d'Oreille Indian, is a good and brave man, and is well thought of among his people. He is an excellent guide in the mountains where his tribe resides.

Choits-Kan. (Indian name.)

THE BROKEN LEG

The Broken Leg (English name)
Kou-sheene, of the best and principal men of the Pend d'Oreille Indians is noted for his proud character and noble generosity. From having given numerous presents to his tribe, he is now poor. He is noted particularly among his tribe for the numerous feasts he makes his people and the many presents he bestows upon the poor. He is about forty years old.

Kou-sheene. (Indian name.)
The broken leg. (English name.)

PIERRE

Pierre (English name)
Nu-ah-ute-se, a Pend d'Oreille Indian, is a young but very brave and
good Indian. He was one of a party of five men with their chief who
returned a band of stolen horses to one of the Posts of the American
Fur Company on the Missouri in 1853, passing through the whole
camp of the Blackfeet Indians. A trait of honesty and noble daring
seldom exemplified by any tribe of Indians in North America.

Nu-ah-ute-se. (Indian, Pierre (English name.)

LOUIS RAMO

Louis Ramo
Lt. Mullan's guide to the Kootenay River in April 1854.

PAGH-PAGHT-SEM-I-AM

Pagh-Paght-sem-i-am
The woman of good sense. (Kalispel)

Louis Ramo

Pagh - Paght. sem-i-am
"The woman of good sense

GUSTAVUS SOHON'S PORTRAITS OF IROQUOIS LIVING AMONG THE FLATHEAD

Mr. Sohon's three portraits of Iroquois living among the Flathead were drawn in the late spring of 1854, probably in the vicinity of Fort Owen in the Bitterroot Valley. Sohon's own captions on these drawings make no mention of the religious activities of these subjects. However, the historic significance of these portraits lies primarily in the fact that the men depicted played important roles in the extension of Christian Missions to the tribes of the northern Rockies. Certainly two, and probably all, of these Iroquois were members of Indian deputations to St. Louis during the 1830's in quest of a priest. These are the only known portraits of these men.

IROQUOIS PETER

Pierre Kar-so-wa-ta
An Iroquois who came to this country thirty years ago, and settled here. He is the most industrious indian in the valley, cultivates a small farm raising wheat, oats, potatoes, etc. and owns a large band of cattle; he speaks the mountain french and english, besides several Indian languages.

Pierre Pichette said that "Kar-so-wa-ta" was not a Salishan name. Charles A. Cooke, a student of Iroquois personal names, believes this may be the Iroquois name, Gah-sa-we-ta, meaning Lime or Chalk. An Iroquois from St. Regis, who bore that name, was said to have been in the northwest in 1818.

Of the four Iroquois said to have been living among the Flathead in 1839, only one Pierre or Peter has been identified. He was the Pierre Gaucher (or Gauche) of the 1839 deputation. This is probably a portrait of that man.

Pierre Gaucher (Left-Handed Peter) was one of the two young Iroquois who volunteered to make the long journey to St. Louis in 1839 to obtain a priest for the Flathead. Apparently they journeyed down the Yellowstone and Missouri Rivers, through hostile Indian country, in the company of fur traders returning to St. Louis. Father De

Pierre Kar-so-wa-ta

Smet met them on September 18, when they passed St. Joseph Mission at Council Bluffs. He stated that these Indians had been "for twenty-three years among the nation called the Flatheads and Pierced Noses" (Nez Perce), and that "the sole object of these good Iroquois was to obtain a priest to come and finish what they had so happily commenced." He gave them letters of recommendation to the Father Superior in St. Louis. (Chittenden and Richardson, 1905, vol. 1, pp. 29-30; Palladino, 1894, p. 21.)

In St. Louis Peter and his companion, Ignace, were hospitably received by the Catholic officials who were favorably impressed by their piety and character. They found that both of the Iroquois spoke French and that one of them carried a little book printed in his own language, from which the Iroquois sang a number of sacred songs. Bishop Rosati recorded in his diary that these Iroquois had reached the Flathead country in 1816 (which tallies with De Smet's statement above). (Garraghan, 1938, vol. 2, p. 238, footnote; pp. 248-250.)

After receiving assurances that a priest would be sent to the Flathead the following spring, Peter set out alone for home. He traveled through the winter and arrived in the Flathead camp the next spring, where he conveyed the welcome information that a black robe was coming. (Palladino, 1894, p. 24.)

Peter the Iroquois has been credited with the baptism of a dying Flathead girl on the site later occupied by the St. Mary's Mission. Before her death this girl called out, "Listen to the Black Robes when they come; they have the true prayer; do all they tell you. They will come and on this very spot where I die, will build the house of prayer." In later years the Flathead regarded her statement as prophetic. (Palladino, 1894, pp. 35-36; Chittenden and Richardson, 1905, vol. 1, p. 293.)

Father Mengarini named Peter, Big Ignace, and Little Ignace as the three Iroquois most influential in giving the Flathead their first knowledge of Christianity. (Garraghan, 1938, vol. 2, p. 238, footnote.) However, little is known of Peter's religious activities after the founding of St. Mary's Mission to the Flathead. He was not mentioned in the writings of the missionaries during the remainder of his lifetime.

At the time of the Pacific Railway Survey, Peter was the most successful and conscientious farmer in the Flathead country. Lieutenant Mullan stated that when he left Cantonment Stevens to explore southward to Fort Hall, October 14, 1853, Pierre the Iroquois was the only Indian at St. Mary's village. Apparently all the Flathead were hunting buffalo east of the Rockies. (Report of Explorations, etc., 1860, vol. 1, p. 319.)

Governor Stevens' estimate of Flathead population in 1853, at 60 lodges and 350 people, was based directly on a statement by Peter. (Ibid., pp. 150, 295.)

When the question of the relative fertility of the Bitterroot Valley and the region around St. Ignatius Mission was raised during the Flathead Treaty Council, Governor Stevens called upon Peter, as the most experienced farmer in the region, to render an opinion. Peter frankly replied that he did not know which area was better for farming. (Partoll, 1938, p. 297.)

In the latter part of May, 1856, Iroquois Peter was killed in a fall from his horse while he and his wife were hunting elk. Major Owen reported his death and stated that he was an old trapper who had been a long time in the country. (Owen, 1927, vol. 1, pp. 127, 129.) Father Hoecken stated that the family of Iroquois Peter was settled at St. Ignatius Mission among the Upper Pend d'Oreille in the spring of 1857. He acknowledged that "the death of this venerable old man is a great loss to the mission." (Chittenden and Richardson, 1905, vol. 4, p. 1246.)

Apparently this migrated Mohawk, descendant of a traditionally horticultural people, set an excellent example to the Flathead in agriculture and herding after seeds and livestock were brought to the Bitterroot Valley by Father De Smet in the early forties. His example was not heeded by the majority of the Flathead. Probably much of the agricultural progress attributed to the Flathead by visitors to the Bitterroot Valley in the middle of the nineteenth century was, in fact, the fruit of the individual effort of Iroquois Peter.

IROQUOIS AENEAS

Iroquois—"Aeneas"—
Came to this country with Pierre, but has not the industry or forethought of his "comrade" Pierre. He is poor but an honest and reliable man.

The name "Aeneas" is readily recognized by present-day Indians on the Flathead Reservation as an American attempt to render the Flathead pronunciation of the French name "Ignace." Baptiste Finley, a 76-year-old mixed-blood living on that reservation, said that the Iroquois, Ignace, was his maternal grandfather. Baptiste volunteered the information that this man, known as "Ignace Chapped Lips" to the Flathead, was the Iroquois who went to St. Louis with the party that was

Aeneas—

successful in obtaining a priest for the tribe, and that he returned with the first priest. Sohon's "Aeneas," therefore, was the "Young Ignace" or "Petit Ignace" who was one of Ignace Lamoose's most influential helpers in giving the Flathead their first knowledge of Christianity; who accompanied Pierre to St. Louis in 1839 to seek a priest; who spent the winter of 1839-40 in Westport waiting for the priest; and who accompanied Father De Smet on his first journey over the Rockies to the country of the Flathead. (Garraghan, 1938, vol. 2, p. 238, footnote; Chittenden and Richardson, 1905, vol. 1, pp. 29-30.)

Young Ignace was one of the party who journeyed to Fort Hall to meet Father De Smet on his return to the West in the spring of 1841. "Iroquois Ignatius" also accompanied the priest on his visit to the Crow Indians in the summer of 1842. (Chittenden and Richardson, 1905, vol. 1, p. 399.)

Aeneas rendered valuable service to Lieutenant Mullan's exploration of the intermountain region in the winter of 1853-54. Mullan reported:

> I learned, through an old Iroquis Indian, called Aeneas, now resident in the Bitter Root Valley, whose wanderings amid the mountains had often thrown him with parties travelling with wagons at the southward, thereby rendering him capable of judging of the requisites of a wagon road, that a line could be had through a gorge-like pass in the Coeur d'Alene mountains. Our later explorations proved this to be Sohon's Pass. [Mullan, 1863, p. 5.]

In March 1854 Lieutenant Mullan sent one of his topographers, with Aeneas as a guide, to make a special examination of the locality Aeneas had recommended. Snow prevented their reaching the pass. Five years later Gustavus Sohon made the first scientific exploration of this pass that for many years bore his name. (Ibid.)

Aeneas outlived his more ambitious comrade, Peter. Father Hoecken wrote from St. Ignatius Mission in the spring of 1857, "old Ignatius is settled here." (Chittenden and Richardson, 1905, vol 4, p. 1246.) Baptiste Finley said that Aeneas had two children, both of whom are now dead, and that Aeneas himself died about 1880, and was buried in the old Indian cemetery near Arlee.

The record indicates the Aeneas was of a more restless disposition than his friend and fellow tribesman, Peter. He was a wanderer whose knowledge of geography proved valuable to the Government explorers.

CHARLES LAMOOSE, SON OF OLD IGNACE

Lamuh (Indian name)
Charles (in baptism)
Charles Lamoose—1/2 Iroquois and 1/2 Pend-d'oreille speaks English and French and lives with the Flatheads.

Lamuh   Indian name
Charle   in baptism

Charles Lamoose was the eldest son of Old Ignace Lamoose, the Iroquois whom Palladino termed "the Apostle to the Flatheads." As a boy he accompanied his father and younger brother on the long and perilous journey to St. Louis to seek a priest for the Flathead. He was baptized Charles by Father Helias in St. Louis on December 2, 1835. His brother received the name of Francis Xavier. Father Helias gave Charles' age as 14, his brother's as 10. He also stated that the boys were able to speak a little French, were handsome, very intelligent, and that their mother was a Flathead. (Garraghan, 1938, vol. 2, pp. 246-247.)

Charles and his brother were of the party of 10 lodges of Flathead who went to meet Father De Smet on his return to the West in July 1841. (Chittenden and Richardson, 1905, vol. 1, p. 30.)

Unless this man was the "Charles" who accompanied Father De Smet on many of his travels in the northwest as interpreter, his name was not mentioned in the later literature. Baptiste Finley said Charles Lamoose died in the Bitterroot Valley prior to 1891. His brother Francis Lamoose, also known as Francis Saxa, lived to old age among the Flathead and was a well-known and respected informant on Flathead cultural history.

Bibliography

Annual Reports. Commissioner of Indian Affairs.
    1869-1885. Washington, D.C.

Chittenden, H. M., and Richardson, A.T. (editors)
    1905. Life, letters and travels of Father Pierre Jean De Smet. 4 vols. New
        York.

Clark, W. P.
    1885. The Indian sign language. Philadelphia.

Garraghan, Gilbert J., S.J.
    1938. The Jesuits of the Middle United States. 2 vols. New York.

Handbook of American Indians North of Mexico.
    1907, 1910. Edited by F. W. Hodge. Bureau of American Ethnology Bulletin
        30, two parts (pt. 1, 1907; pt. 2, 1910). Washington, D.C.

Mullan, Capt. John, U.S.A.
    1863. Report on the construction of a military road from Fort Walla Walla to
        Fort Benton. Washington, D.C.

Owen, John.
    1927. Journals and letters of Major John Owen, 1850-1871. 2 vols. Edited by
        Paul C. Phillips. Montana Historical Society, Helena.

Palladino, L. B., S.J.
    1894. Indian and White in the Northwest. Baltimore.

Parker, Samuel.
    1844. Journal of an exploring tour beyond the Rocky Mountains. Ithaca,
        N.Y.

Partoll, Albert J. (editor)
    1937. The Blackfoot Indian Peace Council. Historical Reprints, Sources of
        Northwest History, No. 3. Montana State University, Missoula.
    1938. The Flathead Indian Peace Council of 1855. Pacific Northwest Quar-
        terly, vol. 29, no. 3.

Report of Explorations and Surveys to Ascertain the Most Practicable and Economical Route for a Railroad from the Mississippi River to the Pacific Ocean.... 1853-55.
1860. 12 vols. Washington, D.C.

Ronan, Peter.
1890. Historical sketch of the Flathead Indian Nation from the year 1813 to 1890. Helena, Montana.

Teit, James A.
1930. Salishan tribes of the western plateau. Edited by Franz Boas. 45th Annual Report, Bureau of American Ethnology. Washington, D.C.

Turney-High, Harry H.
1937. The Flathead Indians of Montana. Memoirs, American Anthropological Association, vol. 48. Menasha, Wis.

Wheeler, Olin D.
1904. The trail of Lewis and Clark, 1804-1904. 2 vols. New York.

Flathead Indians Playing Ring, A Popular Men's Gambling Game
—by Gustavus Sohon

James Delaware

Usually referred to as Delaware Jim, James Delaware lived among the Flathead Indians in the Bitterroot Valley after 1849. In 1843 he had worked as part of John C. Fremont's explorations and traveled over the Rockies as a trapper and trader during the 1840s. During the 1850s he worked for Major John Owen as a hunter during Owen's frequent travels to secure goods for Fort Owen in the Bitterroot Valley. Married to a Nez Perce woman, Delaware Jim was an interpreter for the Nez Perce at the Walla Walla and Blackfeet councils in 1855. In 1877 he interpreted for Captain Charles C. Rawn as Rawn attempted to prevent Chief Joseph and the Nez Perce from entering the Bitterroot Valley.

Governor Steven's son, Hazard, described Delaware Jim in 1855 as having "a tall, slender form, a keen eye, an intelligent face, and reserved manners. He was reticent in speech, although he spoke English well."

With his experience in the east and knowledge of the treatment of the Delaware tribe earlier in the nineteenth century, Delaware Jim could caution the Rocky Mountain tribes to be skeptical of the benevolence of U. S. Government Indian policy.

See George F. Weisel, *Men and Trade on the Northwest Frontier as Shown by the Fort Owen Ledger* (Montana State University Press, Missoula, 1955) p. 117-19; Hazard Stevens, *The Life of Isaac Ingalls Stevens* (Houghton, Mifflin and Company, Boston, 1901) vol. 2, p. 69; and David L. Nicandri, *Northwest Chiefs: Gustavus Sohon's Views of the 1855 Stevens Treaty Councils* (Washington State Historical Society, Tacoma, 1986) p. 38.–**Bigart and Woodcock.**

A Jesuit at the Hell Gate
Treaty of 1855

by Robert Ignatius Burns, S.J.

Adrian Hoecken, S.J. (1815-1897)
The Jesuit at the Hell Gate Treaty

Early in July, 1855, hundreds upon hundreds of gaily bedecked Indian warriors from all the tribes of the great Flathead Confederacy rode over the plains and mountains of western Montana to a powwow with Governor Isaac Ingalls Stevens of Washington Territory.[1] The rendezvous, according to a sketch by Gustavus Sohon who was there, lay along the flats of a wide, swift river swollen from recent summer rains. It was a biannual battleground of Blackfeet and mountain Indians, the passageway through the Rockies called the Gate of Hell. There under a clear sky and ringed by mountains, with the prim military tents of the Whites facing the humbler Indian tepees, the Flatheads, Kutenais, and Pend d'Oreilles fought a stubborn diplomatic battle for their ancestral lands. The stormy eight days at the riverbank are known to history as the Flathead Council.[2] The agreement there concluded, pregnant with fifty years of trouble to come, is called the Hell Gate Treaty of 1855.[3]

The aim of the meeting was clear. The way for the railroad to the Pacific had been surveyed two years previously. It lay through lands where the Indians claimed sovereignty. Governor Stevens had the harsh order from Washington to extinguish that sovereignty, to make the

1. Hazard Stevens, *The Life of Isaac Ingalls Stevens By His Son,* 2 vols., New York, 1901, II, 89. Though published long after the event, this work is based upon eye-witness reports; the author himself, as a boy of thirteen, assisted his father at the Flathead Council which he recalls as "unexpectedly difficult and protracted." He includes in this volume a map from Governor Stevens' original and a sketch of the site by Sohon.

2. The official proceedings of the council, recorded by James Doty, have been edited by Albert J. Partoll, "The Flathead Indian Treaty Council of 1855," *Pacific Northwest Quarterly,* XXIX (1938), 283-314. The council formally opened July ninth and adjourned July sixteenth; Stevens was at the council grounds from July seventh to July eighteenth.

3. Charles J. Kappler, ed., *Indian Affairs—Laws and Treaties,* vol. II (treaties), Washington, D.C., 1904, 722-725; "Treaty with the Flatheads, etc., 1855," is the title given by Kappler to Senate Document, 58 Congress, 2 session, no. 319, ser. 4624. The treaty was ratified March 8, 1859, and proclaimed on April 18, 1859. An original manuscript copy is in the Jesuit Historical Archives for the Pacific Northwest and Alaska (this deposit is hereafter cited as OJH Arch.).

From Robert Ignatius Burns, S.J., "A Jesuit at the Hell Gate Treaty of 1855" *Mid-America,* volume 34, number 2 (April 1952) p. 87-103 and 107-114.

Confederacy surrender some 23,000 square miles of territory in Montana and Idaho for a reservation of 2,000 square miles. He had already made such an agreement with the tribes to the west in the Columbia River basin and was on his way to make one with the Blackfeet.

Page after page of this protracted council was recorded to be embalmed in the White man's files at Washington. "Successfully and happily" the council had been terminated, "every man pleased and every man satisfied"; the grateful savage had welcomed a treaty "remarkably liberal in its terms to the Indians."[4] So wrote Governor Stevens. From the Indian side came no documents, only a heartache increasing to bitterness which, but for the Black Robe missionaries over that area, would have spelled disaster for America's troops in the spectacular Nez Perce War of 1877.[5]

Prior to this war, reports of the uneasiness had been transmitted to the Commissioner of Indian Affairs, and among them the Shanahan Report of 1873 remarked with some astonishment the Indians' lack of understanding and bitterness with respect to the Hell Gate Treaty.

> They made many complaints . . . and said they have been promised much but got little. They dwelt much on the eleventh article of the treaty which they seemed to think guaranteed them a right to the Bitter Root Valley. This I fully explained to them and besides explaining it through my own interpreter Rev. Father D'Aste did so in such an effectual manner that they were all convinced of its true meaning.[6]

The secret of all the Indian frustration is revealed in the unpublished letters of Father Hoecken, S.J., here adjoined. "Not a tenth" of the council "was actually understood by either party," due largely to incompetent interpreters. Not only were the words incompetently translated from Salish to English and from English to Salish, but the Salish mentality was completely missed. A particular element not grasped by the Whites was the limited extent of power accorded the political

4. H. Stevens, II, 89, 90. Stevens repeats these sentiments in his 1855 *Narrative and Final Report of Explorations For a Route For a Pacific Railroad*, reprinted in *Reports of Explorations and Surveys to Ascertain the Most Practicable and Economical Route for a Railroad. . .*, Washington, D. C., 1860, XII, book I, 209. This collection of 1860 is hereafter cited as *Railroad Reports*.

5. R. Ignatius Burns, S.J., "The Jesuits, the Northern Indians, and the Nez Perce War of 1877," *Pacific Northwest Quarterly*, XLII (1951), 40-76.

6. MS Shanahan Report, OHJ Arch.

hierarchy of Flathead chiefs. To change the clan system with its individualistic chieftains and to defy ancient usages by placing arbitrarily all under one chief was to court trouble.

In these and many other points of Indian diplomatic history the historian of the Rocky Mountain tribes has few records beyond the Indian camp-talk and garbled tradition, and he is forced to seek his facts on the Indian viewpoint largely from alien fonts. One source however may be exploited as directly Indian: the diaries, letters, writings, and to some extent even the reminiscences of the trained Jesuit missioners who lived and ate, talked and prayed for many decades, so close to their dark-skinned flock as to be almost Indians themselves. Men they were of foreign lands and continental study halls, with an ear long practiced in the nuances of each tribal tongue. It was the privilege of this writer as Assistant Archivist for three years in the Jesuit Historical Archives for the Pacific Northwest and Alaska to handle the great quantities of unexploited manuscript material composed by these early missioners. Research on one problem gave occasion for investigation of the cognate problem of the Hell Gate Treaty. What, from the Indian standpoint, actually transpired at the pow-wow? What fundamental issues were at stake and why were they so misconceived?

The basic answer lies deep within the faded, cloth-bound covers of a tiny diary and catch-all. Elegantly inscribed on its title page with the name of the Jesuit priest Hoecken,[7] it is filled with jottings made in a wilderness mission station almost a century ago. Three and a half inches wide and almost six inches long the notebook contains some two hundred and fifty-six unnumbered pages, protected by a heavy-duty cover of flowered, blue-purple design. Its white, ruled pages harbor every sort of notanda helter-skelter, beginning from both ends or entered at random. These entries are in pencil and in ink, of varying degrees of illegibility. English, French, Dutch, Indian dialects, and Latin are employed to express a many-sided personality in which charming candor and shrewd business-sense are evident. The entries include diary notes, historical memoranda, copies of important letters, financial transactions, memory jogs, lingual advances, rough plans of the mission

7. Adrian Hoecken (sometimes Hoeken) is not to be confused with his noted brother and fellow Jesuit missioner, Christian, who had died of cholera in the summer of 1851. On Christian see *Dictionary of American Biography,* New York, 1943, IX, 106-107.

site, and general records both spiritual and temporal. Taken as a whole they bring into sharp focus a picture of life on the Montana frontier long, long before the avalanche of white pioneers had settled there. Thus we read that "200 balls and powder" have been "exchanged for wheat"; that certain Whites have borrowed four oxen or a trowel; that the Nez Perces, Kalispels, and Piegans are sending raiding parties after Gros Ventres horses—and that there has been homicidal retaliation.[8] Meticulously the diarist records the calving of cows, with the pertinent bovine names. Under date of "1855, Dec. 14," he preserves "Votes for a Couton[ay] chief": three pages of Indian Names each with its votee inscribed at its side (Baptiste won by a clear majority). There is a swap: "1 yoke of oxen and 1 wagon for three horses." Other representative excerpts include:

> 3 frying pans[:] 2 doll[ars] la [*sic*] piece
> Calico 90 cents a yard
> 1 Dollars [*sic*] for scythe
> 17 and 18 noctem intra Crows furant[?] equos ad fort Benton;
>   insequitur eos Little Dog, occidunt unum, triumphant—noctre
>   inter 19 et 20——————— [illegible word] vedet manum Gros
>   Ventres.[9]

Our immediate concern, however, is with a hastily scribbled copy of important correspondence: two letters written in a small, cramped hand, neat but distressingly semi-legible. The first begins on the twenty-fourth page of the booklet, the second on the forty-ninth page from the rear; both are written in French with a sprinkling of Latin tags.

Of more than passing moment to the researcher, of course, is the personality behind these documents. Upon it will hinge the extent of credibility and objectivity in the facts recorded. Adrian Hoecken was born at Tilburg, North Brabant, in mid-March of 1815: two days before Napoleon entered Paris to begin his triumphant Hundred Days march to Waterloo. Twenty-four years later at the diocesan seminary of Bois-le-Duc young Hoecken was ordained deacon and by December of that same year was tossing over the broad Atlantic toward America, there to enter the Jesuit novitiate near Florissant, Missouri. At the frontier boom-town

8. "1 Nov[embri] 1862 [:] Nez Perces, Kel[ispel,] et Pikani furant equos Gros Ventres." And "Hi [Gros Ventres] iterum ad 80 Pik [anorum;] occidunt duos Pikani furantes iteram [,] et occidunt quinque Gros Ventres. . . . 3 februario [,] mediante manu Gros Ventr[es,] occidit mulierem Nez Perces uxorem albi. . ."

9. Little Dog paid a friendly visit in 1856: "Ap[rilis] 1. Arrived here Little dog cum filio et 3— [illegible word] et feminis Pieds noirs[.]"

of St. Louis he was ordained priest in 1842 and, as part of the famous Emigration Of '43,[10] was bidden Godspeed to the fabulously remote "Oregon" wilderness. The next fifteen years of grinding but gratifying toil on the Rocky Mountain Missions of the Society of Jesus were spent among the Flathead Confederacy.[11] He was co-founder in 1854 of the new St. Ignatius Mission among them, and of the abortive Blackfoot mission on the Sun River near Fort Shaw. By 1861 broken health had occasioned his recall to civilization where he was to gain fresh fame as a pioneer apostle of the American Negro in St. Anne's parish, Cincinnati. As late as 1891 we find this indefatigable pastor, his Negro parish now a memory, an active worker at St. Gall's Church, Milwaukee. But his strenuous spirit was wearing away the human machinery; on Easter Monday of 1897, at Marquette College, now Marquette University, Milwaukee, the octogenarian closed his eyes upon a world vastly different from that he had entered.

On the fruits of this toil among the Flatheads Governor Stevens had commented, in an official report of 1855 to President Pierce: "It would be difficult to find a more beautiful example of successful missionary labors." Doctor George Suckley, who as army surgeon attached to Stevens' 1853 expedition met Hoecken, offers an insight into the missioner's personality:

> I walked up to the door of the mission house, knocked and entered.
> I was met by the reverend Superior of the Mission, Father Hoecken,
> who in a truly benevolent and pleasing manner said: "walk in, you
> are welcome; we are glad to see the face of a white man." . . He bade
> me welcome, had our things brought up from the boat, an excellent
> dinner prepared for us and a nice room to sleep in and treated us with
> the cordiality and kindness of a Christian and a gentleman.[12]

10. Whitman mentioned the "Two papal priests and their lay helpers [Hoecken's novice-master Peter DeVos, Brothers Magean and two others for Kansas]." Peter H. Burnett speaks of the two priests, calling Hoecken "DeSmet"! George Wilkes pays tribute to these "pilgrims through the wilderness on a mission of faith. . . We treated them with every observance of respect and cheerfully lent them the assistance of our raft." Gilbert J. Garraghan, S.J., *The Jesuits of the Middle United States*, 3 vols., New York, 1938, II, 291. On their discovery of a valuable cut-off for the 1843 emigrants see Hubert H. Bancroft, *History of Oregon*, San Francisco, 1886, I, 398.

11. Detailed account in Garraghan, II, 305-313. To Bancroft he seemed "nearly as indefatigable as DeSmet"; *History of Washington, Idaho, and Montana*, San Francisco, 1890, 604 n.

12. The opinions of both Stevens and Suckley are given in Garraghan, II, 309. Father Hoecken so strictly avoided speaking or writing about himself that a personal glimpse like this is precious. From others who knew him we find that he had a keen eye for natural beauty; that he had so identified himself with the Indians as to retain throughout his long life in the east some of their mannerisms and

Entrance to the Bitter Root Mountains. By the Lou Lou Fork.

Kamas Prairie of the Pend d'Oreilles Indians in the Rocky Mountains, Looking Southward.

The great Pierre DeSmet, S.J., founder of the Rocky Mountain Missions, speaks of Hoecken in a letter of 1856 as "one of my earliest travelling companions to the Flatheads. He has ever labored and still continues to labor here with the greatest zeal and the most plentiful results."[13] Nicholas Congiato, S. J., superior of the Missions in 1855, reports after his mission-survey of that year: "Like his venerable brother, who died on the Missouri in 1851, Father Hoe[c]ken does the work of several men."[14] The Indians, Doctor Suckley informs us, "look up to the Father, and love him. They say that if the Father should go away, they would die." He is their "kind missionary and friend, the much loved. . . "[15]

A record of his character-defects would afford a more rounded picture of the man. The "potato incident" of local fame,[16] climaxing his failure among the Coeur d'Alenes, would seem to indicate some brusque tactlessness or imprudence. Even if we so conclude from the meager evidence at hand, we are forced to concede a candor and lack of malice in the man. This appears throughout the diary; to some extent we see it in the document here published. A diary entry from another page of our manuscript booklet throws light on the author, recording a personality clash between the two zealous and intellectually critical continentals in charge of the Flathead apostolate:

> Un fall out [sic] at breakfast Against me by R[everend] P[ere, vel Pater] Menet[rey] for the horse given to the chief. My prodigality makes others suffer. I am not master of the property [,] etc [.,] etc [.]

Hoecken's work is admirably summed in Gilbert J. Garraghan's monumental *The Jesuits of the Middle United States:*

> This sturdy Hollander . . . was taking his first steps [1844] in what was to be a long and distinguished missionary career. He came of a family which had the distinction of giving seven of its members to the service of the Church. His brother, Christian, like himself a Jesuit of the vice-province of Missouri was at the moment resident missionary among the Kansas Potawatomi . . . Adrian Hoecken's years in the

expressions; that for one period of six years he met no fellow White except a lay-brother nor heard any news from the civilized world. See the obituary sketch of his life and character by Walter H. Hill, S.J., in the Jesuit domestic periodical *Woodstock Letters,* XXVI (1897), 364-368.

13. Hiram M. Chittenden and Alfred T. Richardson, *Life, Letters and Travels of Father Pierre-Jean DeSmet, S.J., 1801-1873. . .,* 4 vols., New York, 1905, IV, 1228.

14. *Ibid.,* 1277.

15. House Executive Document, 33 Congress, 1 session, no. 129, p. 278.

16. William Bischoff, S.J., *The Jesuits in Old Oregon, a Sketch of Jesuit Activities in the Pacific Northwest, 1840-1940,* Caldwell, Idaho, 1945, 43.

mountains were almost entirely spent with the Kalispel. He was the Kalispel missionary *par excellence*. He shaped the destinies of the first St. Ignatius as superior all the years it was maintained, and moved with the Indians to the second and greater St. Ignatius in western Montana, of which he may be reckoned the founder.[17]

Adrian Hoecken formed part of a small international community at Mission St. Ignatius, two priests and four lay-brothers all from different nations: the Swiss Joseph Menetrey, the Dutch Hoecken, the Irish Peter McGean, the Belgian Francis Huysbrecht, the German Joseph Specht, and the Italian Vincentio Magri. Their mission formed part of a spreading Jesuit network of stations collectively titled the Rocky Mountain Missions and centered largely on a parallelogram of what is today upper eastern Washington, northern Idaho and western Montana.

St. Ignatius itself had been moved that very winter (1854-1855) from a ten-year established but unpromising site near modern Cusick, Washington, to a spot one hundred and ninety miles northeast, near Flathead lake, in modern western Montana. In 1855 it was a relatively imposing cluster of farm buildings, residences, and church. A sketch of its prairie site—mountains looming on the near horizon and tepees dotting the tall grass in clannish huddles—has been preserved for us in the archives of the Jesuit province of Missouri. The quaint little figures who would people this sketch were as international in character as the Jesuit community which served its church; Hoecken enumerates Blackfeet, Spokanes, Kettles or Chaudieres, Coeur D'Alenes, Creoles, even Creeks and Iroquois!

More precisely the mission was a spiritual center for the far flung Flathead Confederacy, a military alliance against the buffalo-monopolizing Blackfeet. They were in all two thousand savages of four major tribes: the Flatheads proper, under the great Head Chief Victor (senior chief of the confederacy as well), the Kutenais under Head Chief Michael, the Pend d'Oreilles under Head Chief Alexander, and the lower Pend d'Oreilles (or Kalispel, though this name is often used of either Pend d'Oreille group); these, not participating in the treaty, were under another Head Chief Victor (Alimaken).[18] Most were, with dialect-differ-

17. Garraghan, II, 305. See also Chittenden-Richardson, II, 444n. and *passim* for details; Bischoff, 224 for chronological sketch.

18. "These tribes are by the Treaty consolidated into one Nation, with Victor the chief of the Flatheads, as Head Chief of the nation," wrote Stevens to Commissioner Manypenny on the last day of

ences, children of the great Salishan family which totals some eighteen or nineteen thousand American and Canadian Indians. Properly the Flathead tribe itself belonged to the now abandoned St. Mary's some twenty-eight miles up the Bitter Root Valley and some fifty miles below St. Ignatius. The two Pend d'Oreille mission stations, St. Ignatius and St. Francis Borgia, had just become the new Ignatius Mission.[19]

To this new site in Flathead Valley, with its "pleasing variety of woodland and prairie, lake and river—the whole crowned in the distance by the white summit of the mountains," over one thousand Indians had gone to make their permanent home by Easter of 1855.[20] During the next few months construction went on apace, fields were plowed and sowed, plans were evolved to secure goods from St. Louis via the American Fur Company and Fort Benton. A major event this summer was to be the visit of Right Reverend Magloire Blanchet, Bishop of Nesqually, who would conduct colorful Confirmation ceremonies. True, there were storm clouds gathering on the horizon: furtive Indian runners slipping from tribe to tribe as an ocean-wave of unrest swept from the Pacific coast to the Great Plains; white men preparing to stream north

the council; Partoll, 312. But the alliance in actual fact was a loose one; cf. the speech of Red Wolf, (*ibid.*, 290-291), of Michael (*ibid.*, 299), and of Alexander (*ibid.*, 303). Congiato says of Hoecken at this very time: "He has succeeded in uniting three nations and a part of the Flatheads to live together under his spiritual direction"; Chittenden-Richardson, IV, 1277. The Flatheads proper had been drastically reduced in numbers during the few years preceding this council. The nation of Alexander had been formed from various wandering groups at a relatively recent time. Both Pend d'Oreille groups, Dr. Suckley wrote, "are brave in battle, and are said to be feared and avoided by the Blackfeet"; *Railroad Reports,* vol. I, part 2, 298. Victor was the greatest chief in Flathead history; when he died in 1870 the noted Lieutenant Mullan promised to have the government raise a monument to his memory. Alexander Temglagketzin, or Ca-nacht-ketchim (man-without-a-horse), thin faced and somber visaged, was an "old friend" and traveling companion of De Smet's early apostolate. (Chittenden-Richardson, IV, 1232). There is an 1859 photo of him in Garraghan, III, 78. Michael or Michel (incorrectly named Michelle throughout the Partoll report) "recalls in the midst of his tribe the life and virtues of the ancient patriarchs," De Smet wrote in 1861 (Chittenden-Richardson, III, 964); he is not to be confused with the great Flathead warrior, Chief Michael Insula.

19. There is a contemporary sketch of St. Mary's in Lawrence B. Palladino, S.J., *Indian and White in the Northwest, a History of Catholicity in Montana, 1831 to 1891,* 2nd edition, Lancaster, Pa., 1922, 96; another view in Garraghan II, 312. Founded in 1841 it was "temporarily" closed (1848-1866) and finally abandoned (1891). A contemporary drawing of new St. Ignatius is given in Garraghan, II, 312. On the Pend d'Oreilles see Frederick W. Hodge, ed., *Handbook of American Indians North of Mexico,* Bureau of American Ethnology *Bulletin,* 2 vols., XXX (1907), II, 646-647; on the Kutenais or Kutonaqa, "a distinct linguistic stock in two dialects, Upper Kutenai and Flatbow," see *ibid.,* 740-742. The four nations at the Flathead Council numbered collectively about 2000 Indians (cp. H. Stevens, II, 503, Partoll, 312, and the comparative estimates from 1806 to 1853 in *Railroad Reports* vol. I, part 2, 417-418).

20. Chittenden-Richardson, II, 1232-1233.

into Chaudiere and Spokane land as the greatest gold strike since '49 drew Californians to Washington territory; and distressing rumors that Whites would possess the earth.[21] But the superior, Father Congiato, off for the Santa Clara Valley in California after a three month visitation of the missions, left St. Ignatius behind with the happy thought that all was "going on well," an estimate he probably confirmed when, on leaving it, he passed Governor Isaac Ingalls Stevens coming on to fashion a treaty of peace and progress with the Confederacy.[22]

Father Hoecken, left alone with the four coadjutor brothers, was busily keeping within bounds a small cholera plague, and at the same time was preparing to send an Indian guard of honor some two hundred miles west to meet the Bishop, "when our plans were broken up by a message from Governor Stevens, summoning all our Indians to a council to be held some thirty miles off, in St. Mary's or Bitter Root Valley, at a place called Hell-gate. . ."[23]

Stevens, completing his "Treaty Tour," was getting farther and farther out into a wilderness which was soon to explode behind him with appalling fury into "an expensive and disastrous war—from the effects of which the territories will suffer for many a year."[24] Starting with the Puget Sound tribes and working inland toward the Blackfeet domain on the Great Plains, Stevens had followed the Joel Palmer plan "to concentrate the Indians on a few reservations and pay for their lands with useful goods and instruct them in farming."[25] Five thousand Indians

21. Bancroft, *History of Oregon,* 108, tells us that this discovery of gold at Colville in the spring of 1855 made it difficult for Governor Stevens to restrain his escort from deserting. Colville became "the Elderado [*sic*] of the North" where miners made "from 5 to 15 Dollars Per Day all winter" of 1855-56, MS: James Barron to W. H. Wallace, April 7, 1856, in MSS: Wm. H. Wallace Indian War Papers, no. 16, University of Washington Archives, Seattle, Washington.

22. Chittenden-Richardson, II, 1237; and Stevens, II, 75. Menetrey was probably one of the two companions with Congiato when the party met Stevens on July third, eighty-six miles from the mission.

23. Chittenden-Richardson, IV, 1234.

24. House Executive Document, 35 Congress, 1 session, no. 38, 2.

25. R. M. Gatke, "Stevens' Indian Treaties (1854-59)," in J. T. Adams ed., *Dictionary of American History,* New York, 1940, V. 181-182. See also George W. Fuller, *History of the Pacific Northwest,* 2nd edition, New York, 1938, chaps. XII-XIV; Stevens, with maps and illustrations. The House Exec. Doc. (p. 10) reproduces a letter from Father Pandosy to Father Mesplie at the Dalles telling of war talk which had been the chief topic of discussion since the Walla Walla council, as the Indians plan to unite and fight for their lands. Both Pandosy and Major Alvord, who transmitted this information, were censured as alarmists! Father Joset calls the Walla Walla agreement "a mock treaty, in order to gain time and prepare for war"; R. Ignatius Burns, S.J., "Pere Joset's Account of the Indian War of 1858," *Pacific Northwest Quarterly,* XXXVIII (1947), 285-314. At this time the regulars in Oregon and Washington "numbered only 335 men"; Fuller, 220.

had just put their seal to the great Walla Walla treaty and had then withdrawn to prepare their summary vengeance.

This was the prelude to the Flathead Treaty and to the immediately subsequent Blackfoot-Flathead-Nez Perce treaty. It was the prelude to bloody war with the Whites (from which the Flathead confederates abstained), to a welcome peace with the Blackfeet, and to a most unwelcome land-grab by the United States government. Ahead lay the long, bitter decades to the Garfield treaty of 1872, then the short, bitter years to the Flathead decline. Through all this, and through the tension of the 1877 Nez Perce War, the Flatheads must often have meditated upon the sentiments expressed by Chief Big Canoe that bright summer noon of July 10, 1855, at Hell Gate:

> It is our land. . . If you make a farm, I would not go there and pull up your crops. I would not drive you away from it. If I were to go to your country and say, "Give me a little piece," I wonder would you say, "Here, take it." . . I am very poor. This is all the small piece I have got. I am not going to let it go.[26]

On Sunday, June 24, 1855, Stevens had reached Sacred Heart Mission among the Coeur d'Alenes. After a conference with the chiefs on Tuesday, he left "the most cordial and hospitable" Jesuits.[27] A summer storm delayed him for two days in his next camp, where a Flathead arrived to say that "all were looking forward to the council."[28] On Friday he forded the Coeur d'Alene River at sixteen different places, and paused to exchange a few words with Father Congiato, S.J., and his companions who were returning from the Bitter Root Valley. That Sunday a Coeur d'Alene Indian, who had been dispatched some days previously to the Bitter Root Valley, returned with a message from Special Agent Adams: "everything is quiet in the Indian country" and the Flathead tribes are ready to assemble.[29] The whole of July fourth, the day Hoecken started for Hell Gate, Stevens spent floundering one hundred and fifty yards across the swollen Bitter Root; a nearby Flathead

---

26. Stevens, II, 90; cf. the Partoll version, 291-295. The Pend d'Oreille Big Canoe (1799-1882) was noted as a staunch friend of the Whites.

27. I. I. Stevens' *Narrative* of 1855, *Railroad Reports*, vol. XII, book I, 201.

28. *Ibid.*, 202.

29. *Ibid.*, 203. Thomas Adams, a Stevens aide and artist on the 1853 explorations, was Special Indian Agent for the Flatheads from 1854; see H. Stevens, I, 306, II, 75, 92; Bancroft, *History of Montana*, 102 n. Stevens had promised the Flatheads a council and treaty two years before, during an informal council at St. Mary's in the Bitter Root Valley, September 30 and October 1, 1853.

group, unencumbered with a pack train, did it in an hour! While Hoecken waited impatiently at Hell Gate the next day, Stevens delayed almost until noon before he broke camp and journeyed eighteen miles up the right bank of the river. A Flathead brought a note from Adams "saying that the Indians were patiently waiting for my arrival."[30] Stevens sent assurances to Adams that he would be there next day, but the agent apparently neglected to tell Hoecken. Early on the seventh, when the Jesuit was already back at the mission, Stevens met the Indian vanguard and soon established camp for his small band of twenty-one.

The official record of what followed transmits the Indian thought only crudely at best, often garbling it to the point of unintelligibility. With Hoecken's remarks to guide us as to the intent of certain speeches, however, we may draw from these notes of the proceedings the official picture of the council.

The afternoon of his arrival the governor was host to the three head chiefs at an informal conference. After the usual prolonged puffing of tobacco, to signify mutual friendship, Stevens outlined his plan for a reservation and formally invited the chiefs to the council; he solemnly promised that the proposed treaty with the Blackfeet would keep that tribe "out of this valley, and if that will not do it we will then have soldiers who will."[31] Chief Victor announced that twelve of his peaceful hunters had been killed by raiding Blackfeet recently, and many horses stolen. "I would have had my revenge ere this," he said, had it not been for fear of White soldiers.[32]

At one-thirty on Monday afternoon, July ninth, Stevens and six assistants met the assembled braves in formal council. The governor regretted that Victor of the lower Pend d'Oreilles would not attend the council; he wished all four nations to act as one nation, selling to the Great Father in Washington all their lands except a tract large enough for their cattle and farms. In return the Whites offered a hospital with resident physician, and for twenty years a farmer, a blacksmith, a wheelwright, a saw mill, a grist mill, and a school. Each Indian was to receive "a large amount" of "everything to start your farms"—with more

---

30. Stevens, *Narrative* of 1855, 207.
31. Partoll, 285.
32. *Ibid.*, 286.

of each necessary item yearly for twenty years.[33] Their tribal law was to be respected. The Black Robes were mentioned, not without implied criticism. Stevens mistrusted their influence, as the event was to prove.

> We look with favor on the missionaries that come amongst the Indians where they desire them and I think their coming may do them good. The priest will be your friend, but he will not have control whatever over your affairs. The priest will advise you in your spiritual affairs— that which relates to God, but he will have no control over your temporal affairs, your own laws; that you will manage yourself.[34]

Victor replied that he had confidence in Stevens' good intentions, but that he could not give the Whites a large piece of land since he had very little. Alexander touched briefly on hell, God, man's final purpose, and his people's undisciplined character; perhaps fear of the Whites would supply what the priestly exhortations lacked. "The priest instructs me and these people here," Alexander concluded; "I am very well content with the priest and am very well satisfied with you."[35] The Flathead Red Wolf then protested that all this talk of one nation, where before there had been three, was confusing.

The following afternoon Chief Big Canoe delivered one of the longest and most poignant speeches of the council.[36] He could not understand the need for a treaty since there had been no war; his people had never spilt a drop of White blood. At great cost to his tribe he has humored the Whites by calling back war parties who wished revenge against the Blackfeet. "I am quiet and sit down on my land," he protested; "I thought nobody would talk about land, would trouble me." For his part, he would never go to the White man's country and impose on them this way. This is his country; he grew up here; he is poor and wants to keep his land. He wishes the Whites to go away to their own country. The White men talk "so smoothly, so well"; they "just talk as they please" to the poor Indian.

---

33. *Ibid.*, 288. Most of these things had already been made available to these tribes by the Jesuits. Thus Suckley reports at the old St. Ignatius Mission in 1853: pigs, poultry, cattle, agricultural implements, tools, a windmill, blacksmith shop and carpenter shop (served by lay-brothers), barns, cow-sheds, houses, a one hundred and sixty acre mission farm, Indian houses; he also tells how this community makes its own ploughshares, tobacco-pipes, bricks, candles, etc. Garraghan, II, 310.

34. Partoll, 288.

35. *Ibid.*, 290.

36. *Ibid.*, 291-295. On Big Canoe, see above, n. 26. Red Wolf, or Isaac, was a Kutenai whose mother was a Flathead.

But Stevens seemed determined to have his own way. He summarized Big Canoe's speech, framing it to his purposes and concluding that the chief favored the reservation scheme! Big Canoe protested: "I do not understand you right"; but Stevens turned now to the head chiefs.[37] None was opposed to the general idea of a reservation, though Victor made it clear he would not leave his Bitter Root Valley. Stevens emphasized the alternatives: Flathead Valley or Bitter Root Valley. He spoke flatteringly of each chief's prowess, painted a dark picture of the difficulties involved in supplying two reservations, and promised each chief a furnished home and five hundred dollars a year for twenty years.

> You will have your priest with you, whether you go to the mission or Fort Owen; and here I would say those who want the priest can have him. The Great Father means that each one shall do as he pleases in reference to receiving the instructions of the priests....[38]

At the Wednesday afternoon session, since Victor still clung to his valley, Stevens exerted every effort to persuade Alexander to join Victor in the Bitter Root. But Alexander held fast to his own land: the priest was there, the berries and roots were there, it was the only place large enough. Chief Michael's non-committal silence was interpreted by the governor as indifference: "he will stand by whatever" the other two chiefs decide.[39] During an informal recess Alexander agreed to accept Stevens' favored spot, the Bitter Root Valley, if the importunate governor "would say he could not go to heaven at his own place."[40] Stevens ignored the irony and urged the chiefs to dwell in common on earth as they would in heaven! Clearly, an impasse had been reached. With singular lack of common sense Stevens ascribed this result of his efforts to the adverse influence of the Jesuits. "It being obvious that no progress would be made by continuing the council today, and that an influence was being exerted by the mission which might be adverse to the views of the government," he adjourned the council until Friday and sent again for Father Hoecken.[41]

37. Partoll, 296.

38. *Ibid.*, 297.

39. *Ibid.*, 300. Throughout the council Stevens spoke too sharply, too self-confidently, to the chiefs. As the Jesuits could have informed him, the Flatheads and Kalispels, unlike the Kettles or Coeur d'Alenes, had "to be treated with gentleness so that one gains nothing by being brusque." Garraghan, II, 385.

40. *Ibid.*

41. *Ibid.* This was a surprising attitude, considering both the religious tolerance of the New Englander Stevens and his many enthusiastic reports of Catholic mission-work. The key to this paradox

Hoecken appears no more in the official transcript, but Stevens will write to the Commissioner of Indian Affairs on the last day of the council: "I carefully explained the whole matter to Father Hoecken, the Jesuit Missionary, whose presence I had required at the Treaty Ground, and whose influence over these Indians is almost unbounded."[42] Stevens' change of heart after his talk with Hoecken is evident in his further statement to the Commissioner:

> Father Hoecken has labored faithfully among the Indian Tribes for the last ten years, and has gained his influence by energy, devotion and the natural ascendancy of a patient and indomitable will. He has promised to interpose no obstacle whatever to the views of the government, and I have confidence in his singleness of purpose.[43]

Hoecken's absence had undoubtedly annoyed Stevens as much as Stevens' absence had annoyed Hoecken on July fifth. Stevens was to labor under the illusion that the discreet Hoecken now "highly approved the treaty,"[44] an impression belied by the tone of the Jesuit's writings. In common with the Indians, however, he did highly approve the element of peace with the Blackfeet.

Tempers flared during the Friday session. Alexander complained that the governor had concealed the small size of the proposed reservation: "when you first talked, you talked good; now you talk sharp; you talk like a Blackfoot."[45] Stevens taxed Alexander with contradicting himself; he emphasized the temporary right of pasture on the land sold. Suddenly Victor interjected: "Where is my country: I want to speak."[46] Stevens tried to silence him, then tactlessly brushed him aside: Alexander had agreed, and he was now speaking with Alexander. But Victor snapped: "I was talking to you and I told you no."[47] Stevens

would seem to be his annoyed conviction that "so great has been their desire for peace that they have overlooked all right, propriety. . . And the Indians seeing that the missionaries are on their side, are fortified in the belief that they are fighting in a holy cause. . ."; Stevens, II, 228-229. The governor was apparently unaware of the outbreak of cholera which detained Hoecken—a disease which had carried off Hoecken's brother just four years previously, and which the Indians regarded with awe as an "implacable scourge"; Chittenden-Richardson, II, 650; "thousands" of Plains Indians fell in the Cholera Year of 1853; *ibid.*, IV, 1283.

42. *Ibid.*, 313.

43. *Ibid.*, 314.

44. Stevens, II, 85, 90. Of course, he was under the same impression as to the Indians' reactions at the end (see above, n. 4).

45. Partoll, 303.

46. *Ibid.*, 304.

47. *Ibid.*

therefore turned to Victor. Much more was said before the session adjourned but no progress was made beyond this point. Once Stevens openly, though by indirection, insulted Victor.[48]

A final session on Monday, July sixteenth, settled nothing. Neither Alexander nor Michael would hear of moving. Victor protested the loss of his lands, and made an ambiguous offer. Let the Great Father come from Washington and see for himself whether they could live on the proposed sites. He would stand by the personal decision of the president. Both Stevens and Hoecken understood Victor to have made a compromise offer. But the Flatheads themselves subsequently remained thoroughly convinced that this very proposal of Victor's had guaranteed to them the Bitter Root Valley.[49] Stevens therefore had made a treaty hinging entirely on an ambiguous compromise which, moreover, had been explicitly rejected by the other chiefs. He falsely assumed that the confederation was a single nation, and that all would submit to the presidential choice. In cold fact, he does not even seem to have intended any further investigation; that same year he confided to Father Ravalli, S.J., that the reserve was to be in the Flathead Valley.[50]

Stevens hastily accepted Victor's conditions, and each of the three chiefs put his X to the revised document. Father Hoecken signed as a witness.[51] Before the gifts were distributed and the council formally closed, the powerful Flathead sub-chief, Moses or Stiettiedloodshoo, contributed this bitter and significant speech:

48. "Or is Victor a chief? Is he as one of his people has called him, an old woman? dumb as a dog? If Victor is a chief let him speak now." Partoll, 304. Ambrose, Tilcoostay, Red Wolf, and Beartrack each gives his view of the question. But it is difficult to judge the degree of accuracy the official record achieves in transcribing these speeches.

49. Palladino, 95, and sources cited in Burns, "Jesuits, Northern Indians, and Nez Perce War," 45n.

50. See the second of the two letters here appended. Stevens could actually write to Commissioner Manypenny on July 16, 1855, that the difficulties experienced in the Flathead Council had been many "in consequence of the dislike of the Flatheads to mission establishments"! The Jesuits could have enlightened the governor as to the obvious source of his difficulties; they had previously made efforts to have the Pend d'Oreilles move to the Coeur d'Alene Valley or to the Camas and Horse Plains, only to receive the answer: "This is our country; here are the graves of our forefathers; here we were born, and here we wish to die; we do not want to leave our country poor as it is." *Railroad Reports*, vol. XII, book I, 298.

51. In the manuscript original (OJH Arch.) "A. J. Hoecken, S.J., Miss[ionarius]" appears sixth below Governor Stevens. But it is nowhere to be found in President Buchanan's ratified copy (manuscript, OJH Arch.).

My brother is buried there. I did not think you would take the only piece of ground I had. Here are three fellows (the chiefs), they say get on your horse and go.... If you would give us a large place I would not talk foolish. If I go in your country and say give me this, will you give it me. May be you do know it . . . they have only one piece of ground.
. . Last year when you were talking about the Blackfeet you were joking.[52]

The Jesuits aided Stevens more than once during his Treaty Tour, but the real Jesuit contribution to this Flathead treaty was to come after Stevens had departed. Having "bought" the vast Indian holdings, the United States government did not pay for them. The money, the tools, the school and hospital, the blacksmith—all the grand promises came to nothing. The all-important presidential survey was forgotten until 1872, by which time White settlement had already reached the Bitter Root Valley.[53] Nevertheless the government had the effrontery to request the struggling Jesuits themselves to make the payment![54] They did so, but it was simply a continuation of the splendid work they had been doing for fifteen years. Nine months after the Flathead Council, Father Hoecken wrote to Father De Smet in St. Louis:

> Here in our missions, we already observe all the conditions stipulated in the treaty concluded last year by Governor Stevens, at Hellgate. Our brothers assist the Indians, and teach them how to cultivate the ground. They distribute the fields and the seeds for sowing and planting, as well as the plows and other agricultural instruments. Our blacksmith works for them: he repairs their guns, their axes, their knives; the carpenter renders them great assistance in constructing their houses . . . our little mill is daily in use for

52. Partoll, 310. Moses was the baptismal name given to Stiettiedloodshoo by Father De Smet who was his "adopted Indian brother." He was a powerful Flathead sub-chief whose surname meant "Bravest-of-the-Brave." De Smet tells us he was "distinguished by his superior skill in horsemanship," and "the handsomest Indian warrior of my acquaintance." Chittenden-Richardson, I, 305, II, 472, 576, 766, IV, 1225, 1240. According to the official version of his speech, Moses understood the transaction in the same sense as Stevens wished, and rejected it; however, even Stevens realized that Michael and Alexander had not agreed to move (Partoll, 313), and so this element of the speech may be badly recorded.

53. In a letter written less than a year after the treaty Hoecken mentions "the Whites, the number of whom is daily augmenting in St. Mary's valley"; Chittenden-Richardson, IV, 1240; by 1877 there would be 450 Whites in the Bitter Root Valley. Steven's initial error was compounded by the disgraceful Garfield Treaty of 1872: the name of the Flathead head chief was simply forged to the instrument which was sent to the Senate for approval; when the head chief still stood firm, the government set up its own puppet regime and enforced the treaty as best it could. In 1883 an investigating Senate Subcommittee exposed the fraud.

54. Palladino, 96.

grinding their grain . . . in a word, all we have and all we are is sacrificed to the welfare of the Indian. The savings that our religious economy enables us to make . . . is theirs! Through love of Jesus Christ we are ready to sacrifice all, even life itself.[55]

And in the same letter, Hoecken proposes a reservation idea, much more magnanimous than the government's, which he feels could be effected:

Were I authorized to suggest a plan, I would propose to have all the upper lands evacuated by the whites, and form of it a territory exclusively of Indians; afterward I would lead there all the Indians of the inferior portion [lower country], such as the Nez Perces, the Cayuses, the Yakimas, the Coeur d'Alenes and the Spokans. Well-known facts lead me to believe that this plan, with such superior advantages, might be effected, by means of missions, in the space of two or three years.[56]

Hoecken adds:

When, oh when! shall the oppressed Indian find a poor corner of earth on which he may lead a peaceful life, serving and loving his God in tranquility, and preserving the ashes of his ancestors without fear of beholding them profaned and trampled beneath the feet of an unjust usurper?[57]

---

55. Chittenden-Richardson, IV, 1245-1246. The agricultural implements etc. distributed did not come from the government, but were supplied by the Jesuits; the government gave not "a farthing"; *ibid*.

56. *Ibid.*, 1240-1241. This plan was not only more just and generous, but it avoided Stevens' difficulty of moving those tribes most attached to their land; the Kalispels were already being persuaded to come to the new St. Ignatius.

57. *Ibid*. During the war which broke out in 1855 and again in 1858, the missioners worked actively to restrain their flocks.

Translations of Documents[58]

I

To Reverend Father Joset, August 1, 1855.

At last—I find a chance to write to you![59]

I received your welcome letter; thanks for the advice. Here are the new assignments.[60] .....

Summons to the Council

After the Coeur d'Alenes' root-digging season,[61] Governor Stevens had written Mr. Adams that he hoped to see our Fathers and Coadjutor Brothers at Hell Gate.[62] On July the fourth I set out with Brother Magean;[63] all day of the fifth I waited for Stevens; on the sixth I started home again. Several days later I got a note from Adams to the effect that Governor Stevens wished to see me.[64] Since quite a few of our

58. The transcriptions of the French version of the letters are available on pages 103 to 106 of the 1952 edition of this article.—**Bigart and Woodcock.**

59. Then at St. Paul's Mission among the Chaudieres, Kettle Falls, Washington. John Joseph Augustine Joset, S.J., (1810-1890), a native of Courfaivre, Switzerland, and former professor at the College of Fribourg, had been superior general of the Rocky Mountain region, 1845-1850. See R. Ignatius Burns, S.J., "A Jesuit in the War Against the Northern Indians," *Records of the American Catholic Historical Society,* LXI (1950), 9-54.

60. I here omit less important domestic details: a list of household duties assigned each Jesuit (given also in Chittenden-Richardson, IV, 1242), a notice that cholera had carried off some ten Indians recently.

61. Lit. "after the Camas." This is not the "variete de pomme" of Larousse, (*Grand dictionnaire universal,* VIII: 977), but *Camassia Esculenta* (cf. Nootka *chamas* or "sweet"), a hyacinth-related bulb used by many Pacific Northwest tribes as a staple food; Hodge, I, 196; missionary writings *passim* in OJHA Arch.

62. Elliot Coues, ed., *History of the Expedition under the Command of Lewis and Clark,* 4 vols., New York, 1893, III, 1071 n., incorrectly says that Hell Gate was so named by De Smet; Chittenden and Richardson, II, 582, mal-translate it from a De Smet letter into "Devil's Gate." Hell Gate was the principal entrance of the marauding parties of the Blackfeet through the Rockies. The council grounds was some six miles west of "the deep, dark portal" of Hell Gate which is itself just east of modern Missoula, and therefore in what Bancroft calls Hellgate Valley; *History of Montana,* 590-591, 626; Palladino, 359; Stevens, II, 77-78, 92-93; Garraghan, II, 264-65, 348. Its exact location is noted on the adaptation of Stevens' map; Stevens, II, 16. Throughout Hoecken's text it is often difficult to determine whether his abbreviation of Governor is "gouv.," "govr.," or even "govt."

63. Peter (?) McGean or Magean, S.J., (1813-1877) of Westmeath, Ireland, one of Hoecken's companions on the 1843 journey to the missions, was the humorous and hard-working farm manager. Hoecken was probably the only priest at St. Ignatius when Stevens' message came; see above, n. 22.

64. "Recois" in the text is obscure, possibly due to misspelling or attempted correction.

youngsters were dying or extremely ill I delayed departure from day to day. And then I received a formal command to appear at the council! I went; Stevens received me kindly, though it was evident (and easily appreciated) that he does not overly favor Catholics.[65]

Lingual difficulty. Treaty terms.

What a ridiculous tragi-comedy the whole council proved. It would take too long to write it all down—ah, well! Not a tenth of it was actually understood by either party, for Ben Kyser speaks Flathead very badly and is no better at translating into English.[66] A treaty has been made or so they will say. The Indians would recount with some glee how they were spoken to at illogical cross-purposes to make a peace (*chemtueg*, as Ben put it). They ask: "What is the sense of making peace? Have we ever been at war with the Whites?" They all show their hands unstained by blood. The upshot of the whole matter, however, was that the governor wanted the Flatheads, the Pend d'Oreilles, the Kutenais, and the Kalispels in one place. Where, you ask? Absurdly enough, farther up the Flathead valley,[67] some fifteen miles above the abandoned St. Mary's Mission. Adams recommended this place both to the governor and to the Indians. Iroquois Peter warned them not to believe Adams; that our spot was better.[68]

Chiefs refuse terms, sign conditionally

Chief Victor was for the land his tribe now holds. Chiefs Alexander and Michael favor the St. Ignatius area.

65. But see above, n. 41.

66. Benjamin Kiser (sometimes Keiser) was a half-breed Shawnee who, with Sohon, served as interpreter at both the Flathead and Blackfoot Councils. Later he was a trader and rancher in western Montana. Stevens, II, 92, 115, 117; Partoll, 287n.

67. The Bitter Root Valley; Hoecken either errs in the name, though not in the description, or else simply wishes to designate that valley which is the home of Victor's Flatheads. Cp. Partoll, 300, where Stevens says: "not having agreed I say both go above Ft. Owen; that is the best place."

68. But in the open council Peter was non-committal; Partoll, 297. Peter is Pierre Gauche or Gaucher or Left-Handed Peter, a "venerable old man" who would die within the next year or two years; cf. De Smet, *Western Missions and Missionaries. . .*, New York, 1859, 316. He had been one of the twelve (D'Aste MS in OJH Arch.) or twenty-four, according to Bishop Rosati, (in Palladino, 29) Iroquois employees of the Hudson's Bay Company who had settled among the Flatheads. After twenty-three years with this tribe Peter accompanied Young Ignace on the third of the many Flathead attempts to secure a priest; both deputies spoke French, and received the sacrament of Confirmation at the old Cathedral of St. Louis; on this, and subsequent controversies see the fine summation of Garraghan, II, 236 ff. "Pierre Baptiste, the old Iroquois" is mentioned by Lieutenant Mullan; House Exec. Doc., 33rd Cong., 312, and by Doctor Suckley; *ibid.*, 278.

One day tragedy interrupts the comedy. Victor being called an old woman and a dog by the governor, or at least by his interpreter, leaves the council and retires to his tent. Chief Alexander calls the governor two-faced and a treacherous Blackfoot.[69] What an ending!

Victor wants the government to pass judgment on both sites, and he will then choose accordingly. If our place is judged better he will come here. Alexander and Michael have refused point-blank to go elsewhere. On that understanding, the Indians have signed the treaty.[70] Will they get something more? Who knows? The governor asked Alexander if he would like a flour-mill, a sawmill, a farmer, a blacksmith, a school teacher? To each question he answered no, considering that they already possessed all these.[71]

Stevens suspects Hoecken

I had nothing to do with all this; never was religion spoken of by either side.[72] However, the governor before leaving told me: "Father, your influence with the Indians is very strong. It is on account of you that the savages cling to their lands." He had already said the same to Chief Alexander: "You love your priests; that is why you won't give in." Alexander retorted: "I love my lands. I do not love the Fathers.[73] Years ago when the priests were at St. Mary's, I lived on my own lands."

Blackfoot treaty; conclusion

But more of this later, for I intend to follow Father Menetrey's suggestion and go down to St. Paul's Mission, there to make my Retreat,

69. Partoll, 308, mentions Victor's departure but misses its significance. On the incident as reported in Partoll, see above, n. 48.

70. I have filled out the abbreviation "gouv." here to mean not governor but government (i.e. federal): cf. parallel passage in Letter II. "The Indians," writes Hoecken to De Smet two years later, "appear . . . very reluctant to part with their lands; they will scarcely hear of the depositions to be taken"; Chittenden-Richardson, IV, 1240. The next sentence of French text is somewhat obscure in the manuscript; I have reconstructed it as best I could.

71. The Partoll transcript does not include this. The refusal may not have been understood, or not recorded, or perhaps it was only part of Friday's angry interchange.

72. Hoecken must mean that he took no part in the discussions, since he did sign as witness. Religion was indeed spoken of by both sides, but Hoecken may refer either to the treaty itself or, more probably, to the deliberate segregation here by Stevens of moral, religious, and socio-religious affairs from the Indians' public affairs. Hoecken seems to say, therefore, that his cooperation was negative; the Indians made up their own minds, and he stood in the way of neither party.

73. See below, n. 81. This is not in Partoll's text, but perhaps we may place it in the Wednesday session after Alexander and Stevens had reached their impasse, and before Hoecken was sent for. In this session Alexander had mentioned the mission establishment ("the priest") as one reason for clinging to his valley. He would probably then have had to deny to the suspicious Stevens any influence by Hoecken on his decision.

unless some serious obstacle arises.[74] In a few days everyone will have gone off on their annual buffalo hunt in accordance with the peace treaty.[75] Only a few will be left here until autumn.

....

By the way; the governor wants the Coeur d'Alenes here, or else with the Chaudieres on a reservation among the Yakimas—Catholics with Catholics. The Protestant (as he conceives it) Spokanes he wishes to be with the Protestant Nez Perces.[76]

Should your reverence not approve of this project, send your reply through the Coeur d'Alene Mission. From there, then, I shall be returning with goods which must have arrived there from the country below.[77]

[unsigned]

74. Pere Joseph Menetrey (1812-1891) was superintendent of material needs under the mission superior Hoecken; on his life and work see Palladino, 179-180, and Bischoff, 277, a complete chronological sketch of his career. The "retreat" here referred to is probably the famed *Spiritual Exercises* of Ignatius Loyola. "S[aint] Paul, ou Colville, ou les Chaudieres" appears on Joset's 1849 sketch-map in the Jesuit Central Archives at Rome as thirteen days' journey northwest of old St. Mary's, six days from the Coeur d'Alene mission, and two days above the "old St. Ignatius"; Garraghan, II, 312-313.

75. On the Blackfoot treaty and Hoecken's role therein, see below n. 84. A total of 16,000 Indians were party to this agreement, misrepresented by Bancroft (*History of Montana,* 102) as a Nez Perce-Blackfoot affair. Details are in Stevens, II, 32-33. With the next sentence of our document I omit the major part of a page—details of the contemplated St. Paul's trip (he will pass the Coeur d'Alene mission and return at the beginning of October).

76. For the Coeur d'Alenes, an important Salish people centering on Lake Coeur d'Alene in modern north Idaho, see Hodge II, 594. The Chaudieres or Shuyelpi (Skoyelpy) are a Salish group between Kettle Falls and the Spokane river; *ibid.,* I, 326-327. The Yakimas, a Shahaptian nation, would be leaders in the 1855 war; *ibid.,* II, 983-984 on location and history. The Shahaptian Nez Perces (*ibid.,* II, 65-67) were Protestant or pagan with a handful of notable exceptions until Cataldo's evangelizing in the sixties; the Salish Spokanes (*ibid.,* II, 625), several different tribes along the Spokane River, would be Protestant in the main for some time to come, despite Hoecken's qualifying "comme il dit"; MS: TS, H. T. Cowley reminiscences, University of Washington Archives, Seattle, Washington. In 1849, however, Hoecken wrote to the Jesuit General at Rome that in desires the Spokanes were divided, some wanting Catholic missioners, others Protestant; Garraghan, II, 340 and n. Stevens wrote in his report on the 1853 explorations: "Nearly all the Indians east of the Cascades are sincere Christians, mostly Catholics; but the Spokanes and a part of the Nez Perces are Protestants." *Railroad Reports,* vol. I, part 2, 147. "The only missions now among the eastern tribes are those of the Jesuits and Oblat[e]s"; *ibid.,* 422. In the French text, if the "ou" be "un" a variant translation must of course be supplied.

77. From Fort Vancouver, or the Hudson's Bay Post Walla Walla, soon after destroyed by war. Goods could also be gotten at the Hudson's Bay Company Fort Colville, or from far-away Fort Benton on the Missouri. Coeur d'Alene Mission (the old site, near modern Cataldo, Idaho) was six days' semi-desert hardship from Fort Walla Walla, and seven added days from Fort Vancouver. The antecedent for the French "plan" in our preceding sentence may be the reservation for the Catholic Indians, but probably is the projected trip and retreat.

II

January 10, 1856

Reverend and Dear Father Superior.[78]

One of the greatest privations I sustain here, is to be exiled so terribly far from a Father Superior. Of his kind support I feel almost continual need.

In answer to your request, and to discover what you wish us to do (and at the same time for my own spiritual solace) I begin this letter. When I shall be able to have it effectively delivered, God alone knows.[79]

Summons to the Council

Several days after you left us, Mr. Adams who is a sort of agent for these Indians came here to invite us all to a council at which, on July the fourth, a treaty was to be drawn up between Governor Stevens and the Pend d'Oreilles, Kutenais, and Flatheads. I set out with Brother Magean. The governor was not there. Annoyed, we waited for him over the fifth of July and on the sixth went back home, for time was too precious to waste.

On the tenth Adams sent a note saying that the governor desires to see me. Five or six children, however, were dangerously ill of some kind of cholera. I kept a horse in readiness for two nights to go to see the governor should the children improve. But then I received a letter (which I enclose) from the governor. I went to him on the morrow. He received me, outwardly at least, with all kindness. But I do not understand why he summoned me; the treaty was none of my affair.

---

78. Nicholas Congiato (1816-1897) was a Sardinian Jesuit of exceptional administrative talent. Fleeing Italy during the 1848 troubles he completed his sacerdotal studies at Bardstown, Kentucky, where he became rector of St. Joseph's College. From 1854 to 1858 he was superior general of the California and Rocky Mountain missions, and after 1858 of the latter mission alone for three years. He is noted for his peace services in the 1858 Coeur d'Alene war, and as the founder of the Jesuit house of studies at Los Gatos, California. At the time of this letter he had just completed a three-month visitation of the mission, leaving St. Ignatius as Stevens approached.

79. The letter would be sent to the Santa Clara valley in California. Six years earlier Joset had complained to the Jesuit General at Rome that: "From Superiors . . . we hardly get an answer in eighteen months. Even with resident members of the Mission, correspondence is very slow." Even between St. Mary's and St. Ignatius delivery of letters was had only "three or four times a year." Garraghan, II, 359.

Hoecken and the double-reserve plan

None of the Indians would hear of *selling* their lands. Finally Governor Stevens suggested two reservations, one extending from Lolo fork to a spot some miles above our abandoned St. Mary's Mission, the other running from here on up to the lake higher in the north. The business was all but over; the reserve would have been given them, even though the Pend d'Oreilles and Kutenais rejected it. Perhaps the governor hoped I would side with him, but that would have been against my conscience, convinced as I was that the designated area was unsuitable for the Flatheads and especially for the Kalispels. Dear God! It would have meant the end of Mission St. Ignatius!

Victor's solution

Finally, the "insignificant" Victor, who had been mocked as a woman and a dog the day before (and who is called the head chief of the Flathead Confederacy) moved that the two reserves be examined by the President of the United States;[80] and he promised to follow the president's judgment in making his own choice. Alexander, chief of the Pend d'Oreilles, and Michael, chief of the Kutenais, absolutely refused to accept any reserve other than that proposed on their own lands, even should the president decide that the other was better. One day the governor told them: "It is because you have priests that you cling to your land." Alexander answered him: "No, I do not love the priests (a *mendacium officiosum*)[81] but I do love my lands." The treaty was concluded upon that condition: the two reservations were to be investigated by the president. However, the governor has since conceded to Father Ravalli[82] that St. Ignatius Mission is on the reservation. Before leaving, the governor told me again: "Father, it is only because the Indians are

80. Franklin Pierce, fourteenth president. This passage (in Latin) offers some difficulty to a translator; an example of asyndeton, confused further by use of the historical present, it is susceptible of another interpretation: "Then the 'unimportant' Victor (who was called a woman and a dog only yesterday *but is* now conceded by Stevens to be master of the confederacy), mollified, proposes that the two reserves be examined . . ." Cf. Partoll, above, n. 48.

81. L. for "officious lie." In moral theology lies may be classified as malicious, jocose, or officious. The last is one "of necessary or excuse . . . told for one's own or another's advantage"; in itself and prescinding from qualifying circumstances its guilt is considered rather venial than grave.

82. A significant admission by Stevens, nullifying from the start article XI of the treaty. Anthony Ravalli, S.J., (1812-1884) was an Italian priest then among the Coeur d'Alenes. Of artistic, medical, and mechanical talents, he is remembered as a pioneer doctor, builder of the famed "church built without nails" for the Coeur d'Alenes, and peace maker in the 1855 war. Ravalli County in Montana is named for him. Ravalli Papers in OJH Arch.; Bischoff, 230-231.

attached to you, and because your influence over them is strong, that they do not want to come onto the Flathead reservation."

Domestic affairs; conclusion

On my return here we began to put up a barn on the flat behind the temporary church. Father Menetrey is back with the decrees agreed upon during the consultation. Thanks be to God, I try to comply with them. Had I been at the consultation, I would have suggested things which others would not have liked; they would have said that I seemed to have here, without reason, more than they; and they would have called attention to their own needs. Ah, well! Let us forget it![83] God watches over even the tiny birds. On August sixteenth I left here for Colville to make the Long Retreat which I need so much[84] ....

I fear the proximity of the White settlers,[85] for our neo-Christians. Oh, if the governor only had confidence in our Society and wanted the proper means. Then the terms of the treaty could be carried out dutifully.[86]

83. Latin; lit. "let it pass by."

84. I have here omitted, as having no direct bearing on the Flathead treaty some domestic affairs and a very valuable discussion of Hoecken's part in the Blackfoot treaty. It fills some 25 pages of our little diary with minute and closely-written script. Beginning with a request from Stevens for Jesuit assistance at the "consile et traite de Pied noir," it tells how Hoecken follows Joset's counsel, setting out first for St. Ignatius and thence, on October third, with Father Croke and two savages, for the vague general destination assigned. A fatiguing and difficult journey ensued, with a shock at their entrance into prairie country as they met a large band of braves who turned out to be friendly Kutenais coming back from a successful hunt. Then over a "belle" prairie, across the mountains, and "nous voila dans le pays Pied noir," where Hoecken received a musket-salvo salute from "Alexandre cum suis . . . Deo Gratias." Important details of the council are here given; other notes on the 1855 councils may be gathered *huc illuc* elsewhere in the diary. Registering approval of the government encouragement "a la culture des terres" Hoecken began the difficult return trip. In this passage Hoecken also mentions a large group of Mormons near St. Mary's Mission. We also have a journal of Hoecken's eight day trip (from Coeur d'Alene Mission?) beginning August 16, 1855. There is a letter in Chittenden-Richardson, IV, 1276-77, from Hoecken to De Smet from the council grounds. A Hoecken letter of 1857, *ibid.*, 1248, indicates that all is not well at least on the tomahawk front: five Spokanes killed by Bannocks, six of the latter killed by Spokanes and Coeur d'Alenes, one Flathead killed by Bannocks and one by Gros Ventres; the Blackfeet are more amiable, but the Spokanes and Nez Perces are trying to stir up trouble.

85. Besides the Hudson's Bay Company settlers (some Indians, Canadians, and miners) at distant Colville, there were "a few Americans, settled a few miles from here"; Chittenden-Richardson, IV, 1247. A U. S. Fort Colville, established in the sixties, replaced the Colville here mentioned which was abandoned after 1871. On the Whites who subsequently did move in, see the list of Bancroft, 626-627.

86. "Society" in the MS text, is the French "compagnie [de Jesus]," latinized "Societas"; the French retains the original military flavor. Hoecken writes to De Smet early in 1857: "Here in our missions, we already observe all the conditions stipulated in the treaty concluded last year by Governor Stevens, at Hellgate. Our brothers assist the Indians. . . Last year we opened our school, but circumstances forced us to close it. Next spring . . . we intend opening a second time." Despite lack of

The Coadjutor Brothers send their greetings, as does Mr. Croke. Give my regards to Fathers Nobili, Devos, Mengarini, and to any I may not know personally.[87]

ADRIAN HOECKEN, S.J.

subsidies, the Jesuits continued at government request to supply gratis at least a shadow of substance to the grandiose treaty promises of assistance. Chittenden-Richardson, IV, 1245-46; Bischoff, 73; Palladino, 96.

87. The Reverend James Croke, traveling companion with Hoecken to, the Blackfoot council, was in 1855 "a travelling missionary of the Diocese of Oregon" who later became vicar-general of the Archdiocese of San Francisco. John Nobili, S.J., was founder and first president of Santa Clara College (now University) in California, whither he had been sent with Father Accolti during the gold-rush of 1849. Five previous years of Indian missionary labor in the Rocky Mountain Mission had not improved his ill-health and he died, a noted public figure, in 1856. Peter De Vos, S.J., (1797-1859) had been Hoecken's novice-master in Missouri, his companion over the Plains in 1843, and his fellow missioner on the Rocky Mountain Mission. His more distinguished converts included Doctor J. E. Long, secretary of the provisional government of Oregon, and Peter H. Burnett, first chief-justice of Oregon and first governor of California. Gregory Mengarini, S.J., (1811-1866) a Rocky Mountain missioner from 1841 to 1852, was at this time in California, where he later served as treasurer of Santa Clara College for thirty years.

Postscript:

Implementing the Hell Gate Treaty

The confused negotiations over the Hell Gate Treaty during the summer of 1855 and the approval of the federal government in 1859 did not close the questions over the agreement. The ability and good faith of the government in providing the annuities and services to the tribes were questioned from the beginning. The historical record indicates graft consumed much of the annuity fund. Most of the employees provided for by the treaty seem to have actually worked to support the agency, not provide services to the tribes. The hospital and educational services provided for in the treaty were either not provided or were provided by the St. Ignatius Mission with only minimal government assistance. No careful historical accounting has been attempted to see if it is possible to establish the cost to the tribes of this fraud and mismanagement. This postscript concludes with reproductions of four letters from the National Archives which indicate the government did not provide much of value in the first annuity payment in 1860.

In addition to questions about how the government carried out its treaty obligations, problems arose about the fairness of the amount paid for tribal lands. During much of the twentieth century the Confederated Salish and Kootenai Tribes pursued claims arising from the treaty. Finally they were able to present their case to the United States Indian Claims Commission after World War II. On September 29, 1965, the Indian Claims Commission determined in Docket Number 61 that the Tribes had surrendered 12,005,000 acres to the government which were worth $5,300,000 in 1859. The total payment to the tribes, however, had only been $593,377.82. The Commission concluded: "By reason of the disparity between the consideration paid for the said lands and the value thereof, as above stated, the consideration was unconscionable." The tribes were entitled to $4,706,622.18 less attorney's fees and any non-treaty government expenses that could be claimed as offsets. In 1966 offsets were set at $275,000 and in 1967 attorney's fees owed were set at $415,328.89. This left the tribes with $4,016,293.29 on March 10, 1967.

The Indian Claims Commission award was accepted by the Confederated Salish and Kootenai Tribes, closing the legal proceedings. There was however one major slight-of-hand in the settlement: the tribes were not allowed interest on the claim. They were paid the 1859 value of the land in depreciated 1967 dollars. This deprived them of the use of the money for 108 years while the value of the money declined.

The Confederated Salish and Kootenai Tribes also pursued a case in the United States Court of Claims known as Docket 50233. Many of the complaints in the Court of Claims case arose from how the federal government carried out its part of the Hell Gate Treaty. These claims included objections to opening the Flathead Indian Reservation in 1910 to white homesteaders without the informed consent of the tribes and selling the "surplus" lands for less than market value. The government survey of reservation boundaries shorted the tribes of land on the southwest corner and northern boundaries. The handling of the proposed second reservation in the Bitterroot Valley for the Bitterroot Salish was a source of friction for over 40 years and a painful complaint for years after.

The documents and background for the 1855 Hell Gate Treaty presented in this book raise more questions than they answer. Hopefully they will spur further research and discussion.

Questions About the 1860 Annuities

The following letters relating to the 1860 annuities are from the *Records of the Oregon Superintendency of Indian Affairs, 1848-73,*

National Archives Microfilm Publication No. M2, reel 8, frames 24-25; and *Records of the Washington Superintendency of Indian Affairs, 1853-74,* National Archives Microfilm Publication No. M5, reel 22, frames 177-78, 206-10, and 215-17. The capitalization in the letters has been modernized and some punctuation has been added. Superintendent Edward R. Geary's letters to the Indian Office relating to the 1860 annuities are in the National Archives files. None of the Indian Office copies had any reply notations. The Indian Office received the letters, read them, and then filed them. These selected letters can only raise questions—not settle them.

Letter Number 1

Office Supt. Indian Affairs
Portland, Oregon, Dec. 22nd, 1859

Sir:

Persuming that the necessary appropriations for carrying into effect the Treaty of 16th July 1855 with the Flathead, Kootenay and Upper Pend D'Oreilles Indians, ratified by the Senate and President on the 18th April last, will be made at an early day of the present Congress, and as the transportation, from this place to the Flathead Agency of many articles, required in the commencement of operations, will involve an immense outlay, I have to request that such purchases be made by you in the East, and the articles shipped via St. Louis to Fort Benton.

The articles referred to, are such as plows, wagons and other farming utensils, tools for the shops of the carpenter, blacksmith, tinner, wagon and plow maker, and machinery for the saw and flouring mills. The extent of the purchase will of course depend upon the price to be paid, the extent of the appropriation (yet to be made) the number of the Indians, parties to the Treaty, and the whole regulated by sound practical views as to the best and most economical means of carrying out the objects of the Treaty. Upon the whole subject I respectfully refer you to Hon Isaac I. Stevens, late Supt Ind. Affairs for Washington Territory, by whom the Flathead Treaty was negotiated, who possesses an intimate acquaintance with those Indians and their country, and in whose judgment I repose the most entire confidence.

For your information I will state that by the census of those Indians taken by Gov. Stevens in 1855, the Kootenays numbered 500, the Flathead 500, and the Upper Pend D'Oreilles 700, making a total of 1700, which enumeration is reported by Sub Agent John Owen (in charge of those Indians) to be less by 300 than their present actual number.

Very respectfully,
Your obt servant
Edward R. Geary
Supt Indian Affairs

To

Hon. A. B. Greenwood
Commisioner &c
Washington City,
D.C.

Letter Number 2

Office Supt. Indian Affairs
Portland Oregon May 25" 1860

Dear Sir

Your communication 23rd inst with invoices of purchases made by Ind Dept on the Eastern side of the Continent has been recd. I regret exceedingly that the purchases were made without a requisition being furnished from my agency setting forth the articles most desired for the Flathead Nation. I have examined the invoice with care & find it will amount to some twenty five thousand dollars ($25000.00). The purchase could have been cut down one half & that amt. invested in heifers would have gone much further toward toward [sic] benefitting the Indians than the tons of coffee, rice &

hardbread that are now en route for my agency & shipt too at very heavy expense. Hardbread is the last thing my Indians require & it would have been much better if flour was necessary to have purchased the wheat in the Bitter Root valley & had it ground there. You will see by this purchase that the thirty six thousand dollars, the first installment due the Flathead Nation, is over two thirds gone. I fear the Indians will not be satisfied in having so large an amt. of property a great deal of which is perfectly useless forced upon them in payment for their lands without their consent ever being asked or obtained. There is no building material shipt. No irons for either mill & in fact many things absolutely necessary for the Indians have been omitted such as guns, ammunition, kettles, tin ware, &c &c which if purchased in this market & shipd to Flathead Agency at the present rate of transportation which is 40 cents pr # will involve a very heavy expense. One item of the invoice 650 prs Blue Blkts are seriously objectionable, another 120 dzn shawls equaly so, another 1166 1/3 yds. flannel equaly so, & many other items of minor importance go on to swell the invoice to $25000.00 & this amt to be furnished to the Flathead Nation in the name of their Great Father in compliance with promises made them some five years ago. And what makes it appear doubly strange to me that so foolish a purchase should have been made is that the Ind. Dept. was advised from your office on 22nd day last December by letter a paragraph of which I here quote in part, "where you refer to articles required for the Flathead Nation such as plows, wagons, & other farming utensils tools for the shops of the carpenter, blacksmith, tinner, wagon & plow maker & machinery for the saw & flouring Mills &c &c." None of which save a few hand saws, augers, drawing knives, & gimblets, a sufficient quantity in themselves to stock a half dozen shops. Six plows & a few hoes & forks sickles & scythes constitute the farming utensils. Twenty five plows would not have been amiss. How far will six plows go toward furnishing several hundred Indians.

If the Dept will keep the hardbread, rice, and coffee at home & encourage the Indians in farming I will make my self responsible for the result. The Flatheads are not a barbarous people. They know very well that the lands they sold were not to be paid for in hardbread & the likes. Assist them in producing a change in their herd of horses by purchasing them some American breed mares, & a few hundred heifers. The Indians will be better pleased & infinitely more benefitted. The anxiety of the dept. to ameliorate the condition of the Indian is thwarted. Their advancement in the scale of social life is not promoted by the shipment of trash. They may be pleased for the moment but no permanently [*sic*] good results from the adoption of such a course. The Dept may rest assured that I will use every honorable effort to quiet the Nation under my charge & promote the friendly feeling that exists between them & the White Man.

> I have the honor to
> Remain My Dear Sir
>> Your obt servant
>> Jno Owen
>> Ind Sub agt
>> In Charge Flathead
>> Nation W.T.

To

E. R. Geary Esq.
Supt Ind Affairs
O & W
Portland, Oregon

Letter Number 3

Office Flathead Agency
Fort Owen W.T. Sept 21st 1860

Dear Sir:

I dispatch Mr Blake to your office in person who can lay before you in detail the way things stand here in regard to the Flathead annuity goods being arbitrarily held by Agent Vaughan at Fort Benton.

Mr. Blake was again on his way to Fort Benton with the agency train numbering some 70 head pack mules & horses & was turned back upon information recd from Mr. Irvine now at Benton of Agent Vaughan still refusing to turn over the Indian goods, notwithstanding Agt. V. had been put in possession of Sup't Geary's letter of instruction to Maj. Owen &c &c. Mr. Irvine further writes that Agt. V. insists upon his instructions from Supt. Robinson warrants him in turning over the Indian property for this agency only on Supt. Geary's order on him. A. J. Vaughan Ind Agt &c. It is truly unfortunate the way things have turned out. It would have been much better had the goods never reached Benton than to be arbitrarily held as they are. The Indians remain thinking the wagons nearly due would bring them the much needed supplies for their fall & winter hunt.

Mr. Blakes return last evening with Agt. V. prompt & unqualified refusal to let the wagons load with the stores without your written order was the finishing touch. I felt the disappointment I knew it was to the Indians after being put off so long & so often seriously myself. Not a blanket, round of ammunition, kettle, knife, or tobacco, did I have for them. Neither could I get them knowing too that they were just starting on their fall & winter hunt. What have the poor Flatheads done to merit such treatment?

Does the big chief Iron Eyes (Agt Vaughan) want the goods our Great Father has sent us for his children the Blackfeet?

Why keep from us what was promised us by our friend Gov. Stevens five snows ago?

Why don't the Iron Eyes Chief let our agent have our goods when he has our fathers (Sup Gearys) order to get them & bring them to us? Our lodges will be cold another winter our children need blks to keep them warm. In fact I could fill four sheets of just such questions as have been propounded to me in the last week.

The harvest was over. You want meat for winter so my friends & provide from natures hord for your families. I will again write your father Supt Geary for further instructions. Will you write our friend Gov. Stevens too? He promised us these things? Yes, my friends I will. Can we get our goods this winter? I think not the season is far advanced it will be late before your father's answer reaches me. I am poor. Having no tobacco for you I will try & make all things right when you return, &c &c. May you have a good hunt. The poor & I may say destitute Indian is moving off for the distant Missouri plain their great hunting ground.

As things have turned out so unfavorable & so unexpectedly, I will take the liberty of making a suggestion for your cool & mature consideration. That the Ind. Dept. of W. T. if possible repudiate the annuity goods now at Benton intended for the Flathead Nation. Reasons....

1st. They were purchased without our wishes being consulted, &c &c.

2nd. Many of them are not adapted to our wants.

3rd. They have no doubt been purchased upon the Blkfoot schedule & consequently are better adapted to their wants than ours.

4th. They can not be got over until next spring & then at an advance on cost of transportation of not less than 50 pr ct. on account of the condition of the roads being much more favorable in the fall than in the spring owing to much high water &c &c.

5th. A schedule can be made out & sent East in time for such things as are required & brought here over land in due season at a less figure than they can be laid down here for via Fort Benton.

6th. Machinery for mills, building materials, tools for shops &c &c are yet to come & all could come out in same train next summer & would reach here nearly as soon as I would be able to get the stores over from Benton that are already there with the transportation at my disposal.

Heavy expenses have already been incured without any thing being accomplished. I contracted with Mr. C. P. Higgins at Walla Walla to pay him 10 cents pr pound for all the stores he could transport from Benton to this place. In good faith he started four wagons & a pack train and after reaching Benton was refused loading back unless he had your written order.

He claims pay for what he was prepared to perform at least the loading once back of his wagons & pack train although it was his intention to have made another trip yet this fall. I am satisfied you will readily perceive the justness of his claim. [I] do hope you will put me in funds to meet it.

Three of my head packers are getting $78.00 per month. I brought them from Walla Walla with me. Assistant packers herders cooks &c &c. I am paying $50.00 pr mo. all of whom I am issuing rations to. I am at loss to know how to act. These men have all been hired by me in good faith on the part of the Govt for a certain length of time, say until winter set in & the train had to lay over. I have no right to discharge them until the time agreed for has expired & even were I so disposed I have not the funds to pay them for services already rendered. Much will depend with me upon the liberal construction you are disposed as I have always found to place upon acts for the good of the public service. I see no other course under the circumstances that I could have pursued. I have a party of ten men at work on the Jocko reservation breaking land, making rails, getting out timber for mills &c &c. I want to sow this fall the 200 bu of wheat transported by W. R. Davis. I wrote you from Walla Walla that I had made up the deficit from Mr. Simms which can be returned him out of the lot bought in the Willamette by you for this agency. I think but 35 sacks had come forwd. of that lot. The crop of wheat was fine this year but in the smut.

John Owen
(1818-1889)

In conclusion I will state that the position taken by Agent Vaughan has weakened the Ind Dept of this side very much & will do so still more if he is upheld in it.

Every thing has been done within my power of reasoning to have him act for the good of the Service. Even going so far as to send him for his perusal your letter of instruction to me. He has said the house is 16 feet &c. [?] He cant recognize me. Nothing but Supt. Geary order &c. You can canvass the whole affair over with Mr. Blake from which you can draw your own conclusions. My trip to the Snake Country is completely set aside. I have nothing to take them. I had sent them word of my intended visit which makes the matter worse than it otherwise would have been. I do hope you will be able to advise me by Mr Blake of funds being deposited subject to my order with Asst. Treas. W. T. Men will not work with half the spirit they would could they have their money when it was due &c. The portable saw mill turned over by Lt. Mullan I intend having put up for temporary use such as getting out timber that would otherwise have to be hew or pit sawed.

In conversation with Mr. Blake you will have much of the embarassing circumstances I labor under in this remote mt region. By Mr Blake please let your instructions covering the premises be be [*sic*] full & explicit.

> I have the honor
> My Dear Sir to
> remain your obt svt.
> Jno Owen, In Sub Agt
> &c &c W.T

To

E. R. Geary Esq.
Supt Ind Affairs
Portland, Oregon

Letter Number 4

Office Flathead Agency
Fort Owen, W. T. Nov 29" 1860

Sir:

Herewith I have the honor to Enclose Mess P. Choteau Jr & Co's withdrawal of proposition made me in June/59 for transportation of Flathead annuities from Benton to this place @ 10 cents per #.

The agency pack train could have transported nearly all the property in ample time had the goods not been witheld by Agt. Vaughan and the expense I have been compelld to incur saved for the Dept. leaving the pack train a nett gain. I felt it absolutely necessary for the peace of the country that the property should be brought over. I had no funds to meet the expense of transportation with parties here not willing to contract for less than 15 cents per #. I have promised it conditionally subject to your approval. To meet a portion of the expense I was compelld to use money in my hands intended for other purposes.

My position has been rendered doubly more embarrassing than it otherwise would be from the fact of my being so far remote from your office.

The annuities are in my warehouse with exception of six bales of blks & a few boxes of hard bread which I will not regain before spring. How am I to pay for transportation which will amt to some thirteen thousand dollars less what was performed by pack train amting to nearly three thousand dollars leaving me in arrears of some ten thousand dollars now due.

The blankets are far inferior to the Salem Blkts. The shawls & flannels are miserable flimsey things no earthly use. The cott. hnkfs cost $1.50 pr doz. better goods can be purchased in Portland for 50 pr ct less money. The coffee nearly all damaged. Report from Benton says it had been sunk on the Mo. River & brt up by a house in St. Joseph shipd back to St. Louis & then worked in for filling contracts let out in St. Louis for Central Superintendancy. The cloths fall short some 175 yds but the quality is fair. The cottons generaly are heavy serviceable goods with exeption of the calicoes which are in excess full 2/3 rds. The linseys fair only. In fact since examining the goods with the invoice I have no hesitation in saying I could have purchased the same bill in Portland for one third less money. And when I say this I speak knowingly and will submit the invoice to any of four business houses.

I have not examined the coffee in detail but shall do so and I do seriously think it will be necessary to have a board called to pass upon it, what I have opened is mouldy & musty. The sacks from their appearance evidently having been under water.

> Respt Your &c.
> Jno Owen In Sub Agt
> &c &c
> W. T.

To

E. R. Geary Esq.
Supt Ind Affairs
Portland
Oregon

Hot Springs at Source of Lou Lou Fork Bitter Root Mountains, Looking West

Index of Names and Places

M

McDonald, Duncan, 86-87
McGean, Peter, Bro., 126, 130, 141, 145
Magean, Peter, Bro.. *See* McGean, Peter, Bro.
Magri, Vincentio, Bro., 130
Manypenny, Geo. W. (Commissioner of Indian Affairs), 62
Medary, Charles (Agent), 84, 101
Menetrey, Joseph, S.J., 79, 92, 129-30, 132, 143, 147
Mengarini, Gregory, S.J., 112, 148
Mesplie, Toussaint, Rev., 132
Michael (Kootenai). *See* Michelle (Kootenai).
Michelle (Kootenai), 4, 16, 21, 24, 38-43, 56-57, 130-31, 136, 138-39, 142-43, 146
Michelle (Pend d'Oreilles), 16, 94; bio sketch, 99-102; portrait 100
Milk River, 87, 97
Missouri River, 110, 155
Mohawk Indians, 113
Moise (Flathead), 58, 61, 74, 82, 138; bio sketch, 76-80; portrait, 77
Moise, Antoine (Flathead), 80
Mormons, 147
Moses (Flathead). *See* Moise (Flathead).
Mullan, John, Lt., 19, 22, 42, 50, 53, 61, 76, 78-79, 108, 112, 115, 131
Musselshell River, 19, 82, 97, 104

N

Nez Perce Indians, 22, 24, 30, 61, 69, 78, 86, 104, 111, 120, 125, 133, 140, 144, 147
Nez Perce War, 101, 123, 133
Nobili, John, S.J., 148
Northern Pacific Railway, 84, 99

O

Owen, John, "Maj.", 75, 79, 82, 90-92, 96, 98, 104, 113, 120, 152, 154, 158-59; portrait, 157
Owhi (Yakima), 54

P

Pacha (Flathead), bio sketch, 93-94; portrait, 93
Pagh-Paght-sem-i-am (Pend d'Oreilles), bio sketch, 108; portrait, 109
Palladino, Lawrence B., S.J., 68, 80, 86, 92, 116
Palmer, Joel, 132
Pandosy, Charles, O.M.I., 132
Parker, Samuel, 86
Pelchimo (Flathead), bio sketch, 90-92; portrait, 91

Pend d'Oreilles Indians. Not indexed.
Pend d'Oreilles Mission. *See* St. Ignatius Mission (MT).
Peter the Iroquois. *See* Iroquois Peter (Iroquois).
Pichette, Pierre, 5, 68-69, 82, 86, 102, 104, 110
Piegan Indians, 40, 69, 97, 104, 125
Pierre (Pend d'Oreilles), 99
Pierre Nu-ah-ute-se (Pend d'Oreilles), 94, bio sketch, 107; portrait, 108
Portland (OR), 151-52, 159

R

Ramo, Louis (Pend d'Oreilles), 94; bio sketch, 108; portrait, 109
Ravalli, Anthony, S.J., 138, 146
Rawn, Charles C., Capt., 120
Red Wolf (Flathead), 29, 52, 73, 131, 135, 138
Robinson, A. M. (Supt., Central Superintendency of Indian Affairs), 154
Rocky Mountains, 10
Ronan, Peter (Agent), 83, 101-02
Rosati, Joseph, Bishop, 112
Ross Hole, 78

S

Sacred Heart Mission (ID), 44, 133
St. Francis Borgia Mission (WA), 131
St. Ignatius Mission (MT), 29, 39-40, 42-43, 57, 74, 79, 81, 84, 89, 93, 99, 102, 104, 113, 126, 130-32, 140, 142, 146; illus, 66
St. Ignatius Mission (WA), 135
St. Joseph (MO), 159
St. Louis (MO), 90, 110-14, 116, 139, 151, 159
St. Mary's Mission (MT), 40, 44, 67, 69, 72, 74-75, 79, 84, 92, 112, 131, 142-43, 146-47
St. Peter's Mission (MT), 44
St. Regis Reserve (NY), 110
Salmon River, 61
Shanahan, Daniel (Agent), 123
Shawnee Indians, 142
Shoshoni Indians, 79, 94, 157
Sioux Indians, 90
Siwahsah, Martina, 5, 83, 89-90
Snake Indians. *See* Shoshoni Indians.
Sohon, Gustavus, 16, 23, 67, 92, 96, 110, 115, 142; bio sketch, 71; portrait, 71
Specht, Joseph, Bro., 130
Spokane Indians, 104, 130, 132, 140, 144, 147
Stevens, Hazard, 120, 122
Stevens, Isaac I., Gov. Not indexed.